SHARON JAYNES

YOUR SCARS ARE BEAUTIFUL TO GOD

HARVEST HOUSE PUBLISHERS

EUGENE, OREGON

Unless otherwise indicated, all Scripture quotations are taken from the HOLY BIBLE, NEW INTERNATIONAL VERSION®. NIV®. Copyright © 1973, 1978, 1984 by the International Bible Society. Used by permission of Zondervan. All rights reserved.

Verses marked MSG are taken from The Message. Copyright © by Eugene H. Peterson 1993, 1994, 1995, 1996, 2000, 2001, 2002. Used by permission of NavPress Publishing Group.

Verses marked NASB are taken from the New American Standard Bible®, © 1960, 1962, 1963, 1968, 1971, 1972, 1973, 1975, 1977, 1995 by The Lockman Foundation. Used by permission. (www.Lockman.org)

Verses marked NKJV are taken from the New King James Version. Copyright ©1982 by Thomas Nelson, Inc. Used by permission. All rights reserved.

Verses marked KJV are taken from the King James Version of the Bible.

Verses marked TNIV are taken from the Holy Bible, Today's New International Version® (TNIV®) Copyright © 2001 by International Bible Society. All rights reserved worldwide.

Cover by Garborg Design Works, Savage, Minnesota

Cover photo © Photodisc Photography/Veer

Some names have been changed to protect people's privacy.

YOUR SCARS ARE BEAUTIFUL TO GOD
Copyright © 2006 by Sharon Jaynes
Published by Harvest House Publishers
Eugene, Oregon 97402
www.harvesthousepublishers.com

Library of Congress Cataloging-in-Publication Data
Jaynes, Sharon.
    Your scars are beautiful to God / Sharon Jaynes.
        p. cm.
    ISBN 978-0-7369-1610-3 (pbk.)
    1. Christian women—Religious life.   2. Suffering—Religious aspects—
Christianity.   I. Title.
BV4527.J397 2006
248.8'6—dc22   2006001340

Printed in the United States of America

11 12 13 14 / VP-MS / 10 9 8 7

Contents

This book is dedicated to my stepdad,
Pete Wright
He was a portrait of unconditional love
and was adored by all who had the
privilege of knowing him.

Acknowledgments

This book would not be possible without courageous men and women who are not ashamed of their scars, but are willing to use their own personal pain to minister to others. A special thanks to Bob and Audrey Meisner, Patricia Dilling, Marita Yerton, Karl Kakadelis, Patricia Campbell, Micca Campbell, Wendy Blight, Carol Sittema, Tom and Lyndalyn Kakadelis, Katie Signaigo, Melissa Taylor, Blake Taylor, Dylan Taylor, Tricia Groyer, Rod Huckaby, Huck Huckaby, Carol and Gene Kent, Kathy Klein, Susie Pietrowski, Ginger Plowman, Many Nash, and my son, Steven Jaynes. Seeing how each of you has found peace and purpose in the pain of your past has encouraged me to share the hope and healing of Jesus Christ with the world.

Once again, I am thankful for the incredible staff and leadership at Harvest House Publishers for believing in this project. You are truly changing the world for Christ and ushering in a bountiful harvest.

I am forever grateful for my wonderful husband, Steve, for his prayers, love, and support during the months of writing this book and the years of learning its lessons.

Most of all, I am eternally thankful for my heavenly Father for healing my deepest wounds and transforming them into beautiful scars.

ONE

Scars Tell a Story

Let the redeemed of the LORD tell their story.
PSALM 107:2 TNIV

Like the spine of a good book, scars, by their very nature, imply there's a story to tell. They represent a wrinkle in time in which a person's life is changed forever, and they serve as permanent reminders of an incident that, in one way or another, has made a lasting impression on one's life. Travis pulls up his pant leg to reveal where two bullets pierced his flesh during the Korean War. Melanie wears a gold chain just below an incision that was made across her delicate neck to save her life from thyroid cancer. Peeking just below the hem of Gayle's capri pants lies a reminder of knee surgery where a tumor was removed. Showing through Beth's makeup is the shadow of a scar left by an abusive boyfriend's tirade. Just beneath Rachel's shirt sleeve hides a daily reminder of her suicide attempt ten years earlier. Like a trophy, four-year-old Bobby points out his badge of courage on his once-scabbed knee.

Each scar represents a moment in time or a passage of time

when something happened *to us* or *through us* that we will never forget.

I have several scars on my body, and each has a story to tell. One is smack-dab in the middle of my forehead. I earned it in the third grade.

In my early years, I was a rough and rowdy tomboy who climbed trees, skipped rocks, and made skid marks on the asphalt with my banana seat bike tires. My backyard was the envy of every kid in the neighborhood. It came equipped with a drainage ditch across the back border that ran for six city blocks, tunneled under inter-sections, and culminated in a large ditch we dubbed "the canyon." The "canyon" was three blocks from my home. On the other side of this desert wasteland resided the "canyon boys." The "canyon boys" were kids who grew up in the projects. Back then, the pro-jects were an all-white, subsidized housing complex. There was great animosity between the "canyon boys" and the neighborhood boys (of which I thought I was one). On one occasion, the two war-ring factions decided to have a grand battle in my backyard, with only the drainage ditch to separate us. The weapon of choice was not guns or knives, but dirt clods.

Each party gathered on their side of the ditch with ammo piled high. At the sound of the war cry, the rumble began. Terrible words I had never heard before flew back and forth across the ditch. Words like "greaser," "slimeball," "snob"...oh my, how times have changed.

At one point during the battle, one of the "canyon boys" broke the rules and threw a brick. Right about the time it left his hand, I peeked from behind a tree and served as the bull's-eye for his assault. The brick landed square in the middle of my forehead and immedi-ately blood gushed down my furrowed brow. A hush fell over the battleground. Then I pierced the silence with, "You cheated!"

At the sight of blood, the enemy scattered in every direction. My fellow soldiers (or hoodlums) gathered round, fearing I had suffered a fatal blow. It didn't really hurt that badly from what I remember—not nearly as bad as the spanking I received from my mom later that evening.

Well, the doctor shaved a bit of hair from my forehead and sewed me back together. For several weeks I proudly wore a Cyclopes patch as a badge of courage and bravery.

And now? My hair never completely grew back, and I still have a scar right in the middle of my forehead at the edge of my hairline. Bangs have been a struggle ever since.

I have other scars on my body. One is on my right leg on the shin bone. I call it my disobedience scar.

By the fifth grade, I was finally out of the tomboy stage. I think it was Isaac Thorpe's big blue eyes that convinced me being a girl wasn't so bad after all. I got my first set of electric curlers, some Cover Girl misty blue eye shadow, and my own personal jar of Dippity-do hair-setting gel. My mom even let me wear fishnet hose from time to time. But the legs. Oh, the legs. They were scary hairy.

"You cannot shave your legs until you are at least twelve years old," my mom warned.

"Twelve years old?" I argued. "I'll be halfway through the sixth grade by then!"

I felt my mother was being very unreasonable, and my strong-willed child streak kicked into high gear. One Saturday, when my mom was out running errands, I snuck into my dad's bathroom, unscrewed his razor, dropped the double-edged blade into the holder, and screwed it shut. Then I lathered up my legs with soap, held my breath, and took a swipe. *My mom will never know,* I thought.

There were no Lady Schicks or Daisies back then. Only double-edged razor blades that were sharp enough to split a hair. With the first drag of the blade up my fuzzy leg, I scooped out a divot of skin all the way to the shin bone. Yes, it bled. Yes, I still have the scar today. Yes, my mother knew.

I have plenty of scar stories. There's one on my lip where I disobeyed (again) and crossed a busy street to see my best friend... only to promptly fall on a nail, which poked through my lip. There's one on my knee where I ran into a parked car while riding my bicycle and not paying attention. There's another one on my forehead where I accidentally stuck a pencil in my noggin in the first grade and broke the lead off trying to get it out. The lead remains to this day.

But some scars on my body aren't so humorous. For example, there are two crescent-shaped scars just below my belly button. They aren't the result of body piercing, but of laparoscopic exploratory surgeries to try to discover why I was unable to conceive. They remind me of the years my husband, Steve, and I struggled with infertility and the loss of a child. Then there's the scar on my right breast that reminds me of the weeks of waiting and wondering whether or not the lump was malignant or benign. No, not all scars are humorous.

Perhaps the most painful scars I bear are the ones you cannot see. You know the ones I'm talking about. We all have them. They are the scars on our hearts and in our souls. The scar of rejection from a father who didn't know how to love me. The scar of growing up in a home riddled with alcohol and physical abuse. The scar of disappointment at the loss of a child. The scar of broken dreams.

We receive scars in one of two ways: What has been done *to* us by other people or what has been done *through* us by our own mistakes and failures. Either way, I believe that scars are not something we need to hide or be ashamed of, but rather an invitation to share the healing power of Jesus Christ with a hurting world. For a scar, by its very definition, implies healing.

Perhaps you've never thought of the wounds in your life as potential treasures. I encourage you to dig a little deeper, push aside the dirt, and discover the jewels that lie beneath the surface. Like sparkling diamonds, glistening rubies, and shimmering emeralds, our scars are beautiful to God.

Along the way, you may realize that your wounds have yet to heal. That's okay. We'll work on that together.

I invite you to join me on an amazing journey to finding peace and purpose in the pain of your past. But be forewarned. This journey could change your life.

Two

Recognizing Jesus Through Our Scars

After he said this, he showed them his hands and side.
The disciples were overjoyed when they saw the Lord.
JOHN 20:20

It was just a few days after Easter, and I was reading about the resurrection of Jesus in the Gospel of John, chapter 20. I had read the story many times before, but this time God opened my eyes to see something I had never noticed.

In my mind's eye, I saw the premorning mist hovering over the garden surrounding the tomb where Jesus' body had been laid three days earlier. There stood Mary Magdalene, deep in sorrow and mourning over the death of her beloved Jesus. But then... Mary hesitates...blinks, trying to readjust her eyes...and discovers the unthinkable. The massive stone had been rolled away from the entrance to Jesus' grave.

9

How could this be? Mary thought to herself. *Who would have stolen His body?*

"I must go and tell the others," she said as she dashed from the empty tomb.

"They took Him!" Mary said as she burst through the door of the room where some of the disciples were hiding. "His body is gone!"

Without asking any questions, Peter jumped up from his sitting position on the floor and bolted out of the room. A much younger and more agile John followed close behind and eventually passed his older friend.

"He's not here," John whispered as he peered inside the opening of the cave. "His body is gone."

A moment later, Peter arrived. He was stunned.

"Look," John said to his winded friend. "Over there in the corner."

A ray of sunlight pierced the darkness as though it were a spotlight illumining a lone actor on the stage. At the end of the beam lay Jesus' empty burial cloths. Peter barreled past the more timid John and burst into the darkened cave. There was just enough light to see the empty strips of linen and the burial cloth that had once covered Jesus' head.

"What happened here? What does this mean?" they mused.

Peter and John went back to their homes, but Mary stayed in the garden, weeping for her beloved Jesus.

She knelt at the opening of the empty tomb with her hands covering her tearful eyes. Suddenly, a beam of light caught her attention. There, at the spot where Jesus' body had been laid, sat two glistening angels clothed in white—one at the foot and one at the head.

"Woman, why are you crying?" the angels asked.

"They have taken my Master," Mary replied through her tears. "I don't know where they have taken Him."

Hearing a rustling in the myrtle bushes behind her, Mary turned her head. There appeared another figure, as if in a dream. It was Jesus, but Mary didn't recognize or expect Him.

Jesus echoed the angels. "Woman, why are you weeping?"

Mary thought the man was the gardener. Oh, she was not mistaken. He was *the Master Gardener.* "Sir," she whimpered, "if you know where they have taken Jesus, would you please tell me so that I can take care of Him?"

Then Jesus said one simple word: "Mary."

At the sound of her name, Mary recognized the Lord.

After a brief conversation, Mary raced back to the disciples. "I have seen Him!" she proclaimed. "I have seen the Lord!"

Later that day, as the disillusioned band huddled in their hiding place, Jesus appeared in their midst. He didn't knock. He didn't open the door. He simply appeared.

"Peace be with you," Jesus said.

The disciples didn't recognize Him. He looked like Jesus, talked like Jesus, but...how could it be?

In order to convince the disciples that He was indeed the risen Christ, Jesus made a simple gesture. He held out His arms and revealed his nail-pierced hands. He lifted up His tunic to reveal the scar in His spear-pierced side.

It was then that they believed.

As I read this chapter, God played and replayed the frames in my mind's eye, but it was this scene that captured my attention: " 'Peace be with you!' After he said this, he showed them his hands and side. The disciples were overjoyed when they saw the Lord" (John 20:19-20).

Oh God, I prayed, *they didn't recognize Jesus until He showed them His scars.*

Yes, My child, He seemed to say. *This is what I wanted you to see. They did not recognize Jesus until He showed them His scars, and this is how others still recognize Him today...when men and women who have experienced the healing of past wounds are not ashamed to show their scars to a hurting world.*

It was an epiphany of sorts. A revelation. A cataclysmic shift of thinking.

Jesus did not have to retain the scars of the crucifixion on His resurrected body. He could have returned without them. After all, He is the one who put new flesh on the hands and feet of lepers. But He chose to keep the scars, I believe, because they were precious to Him...that's how others would recognize who He was.

For six months God woke me each morning with the same words: *Don't be ashamed of your scars.*

"God, I am not ashamed of my scars. I tell my story with reckless abandon everywhere I go."

Don't be ashamed of your scars, He continued to say.

Like Peter—whose heart wrenched at the repeated questioning of Jesus by the fireside, "Peter, do you love Me?"—my heart stirred with confusion. "I'm not ashamed, Lord. Why do You keep waking me with the same words day after day?"

There's more. Help others to understand.

God is still speaking to me about the power of our own personal stories and how the scars of our pasts are like beautiful treasures. Jehovah Rapha, the God Who Heals, places His hand on the gaping wounds of our hearts and transforms the wounds into beautiful scars. Healing...it's what He does. Telling others about His healing power in our lives...it's what He longs for us to do. That's how others will recognize His Son.

The Power of a Story

My life began just a few days before Christmas. Of course, I don't remember my debut, but I understand that it was a snowy day in the small rural town of Spring Hope, North Carolina. Spring Hope was too small to support a hospital, so my parents took a short drive to Rocky Mount, where the grand drama of my life was to begin. Of course, my life was just part of a series of dramas in the Edwards and Anderson saga, for none of our lives are volumes that stand alone.

I don't remember much of my first few years. I have glimpses of a grandmother, who seemed eternally old. I recall the teeth she put in a glass at night, the big baggy bloomers she hung on the clothesline to dry, and the long thin braid she wound around her head by day and allowed to hang to her waist by night.

Much of my first five years are a blur. Unfortunately, the most prominent memories are unpleasant ones. I am sure there were many happy days stashed somewhere in the scrapbook of my mind, but the dark ones tend to dim the light so that the bright ones have lost their glow.

We lived in a nice neighborhood, with a ranch-style house canopied by 60-foot pine trees. A smattering of azaleas lined the front of our home, colonial columns supported the extended front porch, and a collie dog named Lassie served as sentinel and protector. While the house was a Southern picture of tranquility, inside the walls brewed an atmosphere of hostility and fear.

My father didn't drink every day, but when he did drink, he didn't know when to stop. My parents fought both verbally and physically in front of me, and I lived much of my life in fear. I felt as though I lived on an earthquake fault line, never knowing when the big one was going to hit. There were many big ones.

I can remember going to bed at night and pulling the covers up around my chin and praying that I could fall asleep to shut out the yelling, screaming, and fighting going on in the room right next to mine. On my dresser I had a little pink musical jewelry box with a ballerina that popped up when the lid was opened. Many nights I tiptoed over to the jewelry box, turned the key, and opened the lid in hopes the tinkling music would drown out the fighting in the next room.

Many wounds were unintentionally inflicted on my little girl heart. I felt that I was always in the way, that I wasn't smart enough or pretty enough, and that my parents didn't even like me. My goal was to stay out of their way and become independent and self-sufficient. My parents' tumultuous relationship was the undercurrent to many of my actions and decisions.

Feelings of insecurity, inadequacy, and inferiority were part of every day of my life. I felt that I was ugly. Not on the outside, but on the inside, where it mattered most.

Now hear me on this. Remember, the story of our lives is not a stand-alone volume. My parents were doing the best they could. My mom was the middle child in a slew of 12 kids raised on a farm, and my father was the youngest of six. His dad died when he was five years old, and he was raised by a single mom on the heels of the Depression. I believe that both of my parents brought insecurities of their own into their marriage, and neither one knew how to make a family work.

But God intervened in our lives, and it all began with me. When I was 12 years old, the mother of a friend of mine in our neighborhood introduced me to Jesus Christ, and at 14 I accepted Him as my Lord and Savior. I can tell you that I was never the same. Even though my earthly father never held me in his lap, told me I was the apple of his eye, or treated me as though I was his cherished daughter, I now had a heavenly Father who loved me no matter what.

After I became a Christian, my friends and I began to pray for my family like never before. While my parents were a bit skeptical about my newfound faith, they couldn't ignore the joy and peace I had in my life.

Two years after I came to Christ, my mother gave her life to the Lord. And three years later, my father gave his life to Jesus Christ. I have gone into great detail about this amazing transformation in *A Woman's Secret to a Balanced Life* and *Becoming the Woman of His Dreams,* so I don't want to repeat what many of you have read before, but I do want to touch on my father's story. Let me open the family story on this particular chapter of his life.

Alcohol was not the only vice in Dad's life. While it was never discussed in our home, his bouts with gambling, pornography, and other women were the unspoken reality. He was a tough cookie. But as we began to pray, Dad's tough exterior began to soften, and the thick walls around his heart began to crumble.

After my mother became a Christian, my dad made an announcement. "I'll stop drinkin,'" he said, "but I cannot become a Christian. I've done some terrible things in my life, and I don't think God could ever forgive me. I could never be good enough."

"Oh, Daddy," I replied. "God will forgive you just as soon as you ask. Besides, we can never be good enough. If we could, Jesus wouldn't have had to die for our sins on the cross."

As God began to soften Dad's heart, he did indeed stop drinking—cold turkey. That in itself was a miracle. But there was still a volcano of anger that always rumbled just below the surface, and we never knew when that anger would erupt and spew the lava of hatred and bitterness onto our lives. We continued to pray.

My father had always been a very successful businessman, but sometime during my twentieth year, he began to experience a maze of twists and turns that only God could have orchestrated. He resigned from the company where he served as manager to begin his own building supply business with four other investors. However, his previous employer threatened to sue him and hold him to a restrictive covenant in his contract that forbade him from working within a 60-mile radius in a company that would be a competitor. He was facing court, exposure for God only knew what, and ruination in the small town in which he lived. Buckling under the pressure, Dad was heading toward a nervous breakdown and total loss of control.

Now God had him just where He wanted him. He hit rock bottom, and the only place to go was up. While in Pennsylvania, 500 miles from home, Dad felt that he was about to break. So he drove to a church and asked if there was someone there who could help him.

"Is there a pastor here who could pray for me?" he asked.

"I'm sorry," the receptionist replied. "He's not in at the moment.

"But here," she continued as she jotted down directions on a piece of paper. "Though our pastor isn't in today, I happen to know that Clyde Barnes, the pastor of the church down the street, is out doing some construction on his new church building. Why don't you drive on over and find him? I bet he can help."

So Dad hopped back in his car and drove to a church in the country where he found a man with a hammer in his hand and Jesus in his heart.

"What can I do for you?" the pastor said.

"I need you to pray for me," Dad explained with tears running down his weathered cheeks.

"Let's sit down here on this log while you tell me what's going on."

For several hours, Dad sat on a log with a fellow builder and told him all he had ever done. When my dad finished his confessions, the pastor placed his arm around my dad's shaking shoulders and told a story of his own.

"You see, Allan," he began. "I was a man much like you."

Then for the next few minutes, the pastor unveiled his own dark past and the beautiful hope and healing in a relationship with Jesus. Like the resurrected Christ, the pastor revealed his scars, and Dad recognized the Savior.

That day my dad and a pastor whom I'll never know knelt in the woods of Pennsylvania and prayed the "sinner's prayer." My dad entered the woods as a sinner and came out a saint.

What turned my dad around? Well, for sure and for certain it was the power of the Holy Spirit that quickened his dead spirit to life. And I believe that because this pastor was willing to show his own scars, a man who had gaping wounds that needed healing found the help he was searching for. I often wonder what would have happened if the pastor had been ashamed of his past life and decided to keep the sordid details to himself. I daresay my father would not have accepted Christ that day.

When we are not ashamed of our scars, but tell the story of how God redeemed our lives from the pit, people can see Jesus in our lives. He becomes real to them. Suddenly, Jesus isn't just a man in a book or a face in a painting. He becomes the Healer, the Sustainer, the Redeemer...He becomes real.

Later my dad explained. "I told that man all I had ever done and he said he had done the same things. I figured that if God could forgive him, and even let him be a preacher, then he could forgive me too."

We All Have a Story to Tell

Every follower of Christ has a story to tell. *This is who I was… this is who I am now.* Traditionally, we call our stories a "testimony." In a court of law, a testimony is an eye-witness account. A man or woman cannot sit on the witness stand and tell what someone else told them about an incident. They can only tell what they saw with their own eyes or heard with their own ears. Likewise, the most powerful story we can tell is what Christ has done for us, how He brought us from death to life!

One day Jesus came upon a blind man sitting by the edge of the road. Jesus spat in the dust, made a clay paste, and rubbed the paste on the blind man's eyes. "Go, wash at the Pool of Siloam," he told the man.

When the man washed the sacred mud from his eyes, for the first time in his life, he saw the rays of the sun, ripples on the water, and the lines on the palms of his hands. He received his sight.

It was not the dirt that held the miraculous powers. It never is. It was what Jesus did *with* the dirt that transformed it into a healing balm. And so it is in our own lives.

The people in the town were amazed. "Is this the same man we have seen begging by the road for so many years?" they asked.

"It's me," he replied with joy. "The very one."

"How did your eyes get opened?" they asked.

"A man named Jesus made a paste and rubbed it on my eyes and told me, 'Go to Siloam and wash.' I did what he said. When I washed, I saw."[1]

The religious officials did not like the fact that Jesus healed this man on the Sabbath. They were more concerned with the binding law than the blinded man, so they called the man in to question him.

"He put a clay paste on my eyes, and I washed, and now I see."

Still not satisfied, they called in the man's parents and questioned them.

"We know he is our son, and we know he was born blind. But we don't know how he came to see—haven't a clue about who opened his eyes. Why don't you ask him? He's a grown man and can speak for himself."[2]

So they brought the man blind from birth back in for further questioning.

"Give credit to God," they said. "We know this man is an imposter."

He replied, "I know nothing about that one way or the other. But I know one thing for sure: I was blind...I now see."[3]

You just can't refute someone's personal story.

In *The Purpose-Driven Life,* Rick Warren says,

> Personal stories are easier to relate to than principles, and people love to hear them. They capture our attention, and we remember them longer. Unbelievers would probably lose interest if you started quoting theologians, but they have a natural curiosity about experiences they've never had. Shared stories build a relational bridge that Jesus can walk across from your heart to theirs.[4]

Yes, the blind man now had a story to tell. God planned it all along. Before the miracle took place, Jesus' disciples asked, " 'Rabbi, who sinned, this man or his parents, that he was born blind?' "

" 'Neither this man nor his parents sinned,' said Jesus, 'but this happened so that the work of God might be displayed in his life' " (John 9:2-3).

Sometimes life doesn't turn out the way *we* thought it would, and we cry, "Why, Lord? Why?" And God's response is the same... *so that the work of God might be displayed in your life.*

Paul's Personal Story

The blind man's story involved the healing of a physical infirmity, but some of the most powerful testimonies are of the healing of an infected soul. Such was the case with Paul. He was a man with a past, and he was not ashamed to tell it. Several times when he spoke or preached to the multitudes, he began by sharing the scars of his personal story. While speaking in Jerusalem, Paul began by revealing his past. He said,

> I am a Jew, born in Tarsus of Cilicia, but brought up in this city. Under Gamaliel I was thoroughly trained in the law of our fathers and was just as zealous for God as any of you are today. I persecuted the followers of this Way to their death, arresting both men and women and throwing them into prison, as also the high priest and all the Council can testify. I even obtained letters from them to their brothers in Damascus, and went there to bring these people as prisoners to Jerusalem to be punished (Acts 22:3-5).

Paul admitted that he had committed atrocities against Jesus Christ and those who called themselves Christians. But then he continued.

> About noon as I came near Damascus, suddenly a bright light from heaven flashed around me. I fell to the ground and heard a voice say to me, "Saul! Saul! Why do you persecute me?"
>
> "Who are you, Lord?" I asked.
>
> "I am Jesus of Nazareth, whom you are persecuting," he replied. My companions saw the light, but they did not understand the voice of him who was speaking to me.
>
> "What shall I do, Lord?" I asked.

"Get up," the Lord said, "and go into Damascus. There you will be told all that you have been assigned to do" (Acts 22:6-10).

Paul began by telling who he was and what he had done, and then he told of the amazing transformation that occurred in him the moment he believed. He didn't sugarcoat his past or try to justify his actions. He simply said, "This is who I was. I met Jesus face-to-face, and now this is who I am."

One Last Kiss

"When Porter left that morning to work on my sister's house," Micca explained, "I had no idea that he would never come home again. I didn't know when he kissed me goodbye that it would be the last time or that his newborn son would never get to know him. After that day, Porter never grew older as I had imagined we both would together. Instead, he will forever be young in my heart and mind."

Micca met Porter when she was 19 years old. He worked for Shoney's, loading boxes of frozen food onto 18-wheelers that transported products across the country. His muscles were well defined, his deep dark eyes were penetrating, and the cleft in his chin was enchanting. After one date Micca knew he was the man she wanted to spend the rest of her life with.

One year after they met, Micca and Porter were married.

"We felt as if the whole world had been created just for us," Micca said. "Nothing could penetrate our love. If the world ended, we wouldn't have cared, as long as we were together."

The newlyweds were poor as church mice, but they lived on love and big dreams. Their evenings were spent snuggled on the couch in their small duplex fantasizing about their future, naming their unborn children, and planning their dream home. After 18 months of marriage, their love manifested itself in a tiny bundle—a son. Like a fairy tale, all Micca's dreams were coming true. But then an unexpected chapter appeared in her otherwise storybook life.

"I remember pacing the floor with my baby on my hip, wondering where Porter could be. Dinner was getting cold, he hadn't called, and I started worrying. Then there was a knock at the door.

"As my dad stood ashen-faced, I asked, 'What is it, Dad? What's wrong?'

" 'Porter's been in an accident,' he said. 'We need to get to the hospital.'

" 'How bad is it?' I asked.

" 'I'm not sure,' he replied.

"The ride to the hospital seemed to take an eternity. I didn't remember it being such a long drive before. With every passing moment, I grew more anxious. My mind conjured up every bad thing I could think of, but nothing prepared me for what I was about to see."

Earlier that morning, Micca's husband had gone to her brother-in-law's house to help him waterproof his basement. Porter and Pat dug a seven-foot ditch around the foundation and began applying a highly flammable waterproofing material. As they worked the fumes mounted in the ditch. With only five feet left to finish the project, the outside heating-and-air conditioning unit clicked on, igniting the fumes. The ditch exploded into flames, turning into a blazing inferno. Pat climbed up and out of the ditch, only to peer down and see Porter engulfed in flames. He quickly went back down into the fire and pulled Porter out. Both men became living torches with flames burning their clothes and flesh.

Just a few houses away, firemen were finishing up a call. They saw the flames and rushed to the scene. By the time they reached Porter and Pat, both men were in shock. Immediately, they placed the two charred men on gurneys, loaded them into the fire truck, and transported them to Vanderbilt Burn Center.

"My bother-in-law had been burned over forty percent of his body," Micca recalled, "yet they expected a full recovery. Porter had been burned over eighty percent, both inside and out, and his chances of survival were fifty-fifty.

"I'll never forget that long walk down the hospital corridor as the doctor led me to the room where my husband and brother-in-law lay. Everything seemed to move in slow motion, and the echo of our footsteps rang in my ears. I think I held my breath the entire way. When we got to the door, I froze. Their bodies were so badly burned, I couldn't tell who was who. Their skin was completely black, their heads were twice the normal size, and flesh was falling from their bodies."

Micca buckled at the sight of her beloved Porter. When she came to, she walked over to the bed and longed to hold her precious man. The only part of him that was not burned were his feet. She touched his flesh and tried to imagine him whole.

The next eight days were a blur of visitors, doctors, and prayers. Each day Porter lived was a priceless treasure. As he clung to life, Micca clung to hope.

Eight days after the explosion, the doctors attempted a skin graft to repair some of the more critical areas of Porter's charred body. However, when the doctor approached the waiting room with eyes downcast and face forlorn, Micca knew something was terribly wrong.

"In the middle of the operation," the doctor began, "Porter went into cardiac arrest. His body was unable to withstand the trauma of surgery and he has shut down. He could wake up within the next twenty-four hours. We'll just have to wait and see."

Micca began to wail in deep sorrow as she begged for God to save Porter. She struggled with the thought that it might be better for Porter to go to heaven and leave his body of pain. The doctors said he would most likely lose his arms and be covered with scars if he lived. But Micca wanted him to live! *I should let him go,* she thought to herself. *In heaven he would be fully restored and he wouldn't have anymore pain.* But she clung to the hope that he would live.

No brain waves. No breathing on his own. No awakening. One-by-one Porter's organs began to shut down. He was gone.

After the funeral Micca found herself alone, a new mother, and a widow at age 21. Her tormented heart matched her husband's tormented body. Both were marred, both were burned, both were racked with pain. However, Micca knew that Porter was in heaven worshipping God, completely restored. And yet, could she be restored? Could she continue to walk this earth with the gaping hole in her heart?

I am going to be honest with you. This book is about honesty and being real. Micca was mad. She was angry at God, who took her husband, her son's father, her mother-in-law's son. She felt abandoned by the God she had loved since she was a little girl.

"How could You do this to me?" Micca cried.

Then, one lonely night after she put her son to bed, Micca considered joining Porter. She was torn between dying to be with him and living to be with her son. At a critical moment, the sound of the baby sleeping came through the monitor as if God had increased the volume. "Why did You do this to me?" she screamed toward heaven.

Micca recalls what happened that night. "Just as a mother runs to her screaming child, my heavenly Father ran to me. I did not see Him with my eyes or touch Him with my hands, but I felt His presence engulf me. He poured Himself over my entire being. I picked up the Bible and turned to Psalm 139. 'Where can I go from your Spirit? Where can I flee from your presence? If I go up to the heavens, you are there; if I make my bed in the depths, you are there. If I rise on the wings of the dawn; if I settle on the far side of the sea, even there your hand will guide me, your right hand will hold me fast' (verses 7-10). I knew that even in this pit of death, God had come to say, 'I am here with you.' Through tear-filled eyes I continued to read. 'Your eyes saw my unformed body. All the days ordained for me were written in your book before one of them came to be' (verse 16).

"It was as if God was telling me that Porter's death was not a personal attack or payment for my sin. God, in His sovereign plan, simply knew the number of Porter's days. I was just privileged to be a part of them."

Nineteen years have passed since Porter passed from this life into eternity with God. Micca has since married again and borne two more children, yet the memory of Porter is with her every day. God healed her broken heart and deep-felt wounds. But her scars are beautiful to her, to her family, and to the countless women she ministers to. Her scar from the cutting away of Porter from her life is part of her story of redemption, recovery, and renewal. Satan did everything he could to tempt Micca not to trust God again because he knows that our willingness to place our lives in God's hands will lead to full redemption. Micca has learned that God is always with her, no matter what.

While Micca's scar is invisible to the naked eye, her brother-in-law's scars are in plain view. He recovered, but his arms, back, and chest bare the marks of burned flesh. He always wore long-sleeved shirts and kept the unsightly flesh from public eye. One day Micca told him just how she felt about his scars.

"Pat," she said. "I know you are embarrassed about your scars, and to some people they may be ugly. But I want you to know that your scars are beautiful to me. Because of them, you gave me eight days with Porter I wouldn't have had otherwise. Pat, your scars are beautiful to me, and I believe they are beautiful to God."

Micca and Pat embraced in a fresh flood of tears.

Today, Pat wears short-sleeved shirts.

One Last Disciple

When Jesus first appeared to the disciples after His resurrection, there was one who was absent from the motley crew—Thomas. When he came back to the group, they were abuzz, telling of Jesus' appearance. But Thomas didn't believe a word they said.

> "Unless I see the nail marks in his hands and put my finger where the nails were, and put my hand into his side, I will not believe it." A week later his disciples were in the house again, and Thomas was with them. Though the doors were locked, Jesus suddenly appeared and stood among them. "Peace be with you!" Then he said

to Thomas, "Put your finger here; see my hands. Reach out your hand and put it into my side. Stop doubting and believe."

Thomas said to him, "My Lord and my God!" (John 20:25-28).

The world is full of "Thomases." I was one, and perhaps you were one too. And even though I did not run my fingers over Jesus' nail-scarred hands or thrust my hand into His spear-pierced side, I recognized Him through the scars of the men and women who were not afraid to share their stories of healing and redemption... and I believed.

In Revelation 12:11, John writes, "They overcame him [Satan] by the blood of the Lamb and by the word of their testimony." Incredible power is released when we drop the chains of bitterness, fear, and shame to show the world our scars. Because Satan knows that our stories are instrumental in his ultimate defeat, he will do anything and everything to convince us to keep the treasures hidden away. Oh, dear one, God is calling us to not be ashamed of our scars, for it is by those very scars that others will recognize the Savior, Jesus Christ.

THREE

Reflecting on the Purpose of Our Scars

In this you greatly rejoice, though now for a little
while you may have had to suffer grief in all kinds of trials.
These have come so that your faith—of greater worth than gold,
which perishes even though refined by fire—may be
proved genuine and may result in praise, glory and
honor when Jesus Christ is revealed.
1 PETER 1:6-7

My son, Steven, and I sat on the floor in his room playing rummy. We had just a few minutes before rushing off to register for his summer swim class and wanted to get in one more round of play. This summer was proving to be the best ever. Our golden retriever, Ginger, had just delivered seven adorable puppies, Steven

27

was enjoying his sixth summer of life, and after four years of the heartache of negative pregnancy tests, God had surprised us with a new life growing inside my womb.

But as Steven and I sat on the floor, I felt a warm sticky sensation run down my leg. A trip to the bathroom confirmed my greatest fear. Later that afternoon, our baby died and is now waiting for us in heaven.

What began as a summer full of life and joy quickly turned into a season of great loss and sadness. I mourned for that child for which I had prayed and felt the ache of empty arms. Someone once said, "I never knew I could miss someone I had never met." But, oh, how I missed her. We never knew for sure, but in my heart, I felt that the baby had been a little girl.

During those summer months, I went through the grieving process step-by-step. I'll admit that I was angry at God for "taunting" me with this gift of a child and then taking her away. But through the months and years that followed, God taught me many lessons about myself, about Him, and about trusting in His unfailing love.

I believe that when we go through a trial which wounds us deeply, God can use it to teach us valuable lessons. Some of those lessons are a deeper understanding of who He is, of who we are, and of what we truly believe. Our faith grows in the petri dish of struggles in the laboratory of life. One of my most valuable lessons, through all my wounds and scars, was a decision to stop saying "why me" and to begin asking "what now?" But the lesson that continues reverberating like a gentle thunder is the truth of God's unfailing love.

During the difficult months that followed the loss of our child, I struggled with God. Just as Jacob wrestled with God through his dark night of the soul, I wrestled as well. *How could He love me and allow this to happen? Why would God withhold my dream? Is He able? Is He kind? Is He really there?*

It was a dry summer...in my heart and soul. No one could help me, comfort me, or lift me out of my despair. And while I didn't want to talk to God, He never left my side. Patiently, He waited for me to cry out to Him…to say, *I will trust You even though I do not understand.*

Why Do Bad Things Happen?

There is no easy answer to the question of why tragedy strikes. Is it God's discipline, the devil's deception, or the result of living in a degenerate fallen world? Each one of these is a viable option.

King David experienced God's discipline when he counted his fighting men (1 Chronicles 21). As soon as the last man was numbered, David knew that he had displeased God, and he asked for forgiveness. God did forgive David, but David also had to suffer the consequences of his actions.

> This is what the LORD says: "Take your choice: three years of famine, three months of being swept away before your enemies, with their swords overtaking you, or three days of the sword of the LORD—days of plague in the land with the angel of the LORD ravaging every part of Israel" (1 Chronicles 21:11-12).

This reminds me of the time my son was about ten years old and got caught for telling a fib. My husband gave him two choices for his punishment.

"Okay, Steven, you can have seven days without Nintendo and television or five swats with the paddle."

Steven thought about that for a moment and replied, "Who's going to give me the swats?"

Incredulous, I looked up and said, "Does it matter?"

My husband burst out laughing and said, "You bet it matters."

I guess Mama had a soft touch when it came to the paddle. (By the way, Steven chose the five licks…administered by Dad.)

We don't usually get to choose our discipline with God, but be assured, my friend, whom the Lord loves, He disciplines (Proverbs 3:11).

When Miriam gossiped about her brother Moses and tried to usurp his authority, God struck her with leprosy and halted the progress of Israel's journey to the Promised Land for three days (Numbers 12). When Saul disobeyed and made himself a priest, God took his kingdom away (1 Samuel 13). When Ananias and Sapphira lied about the amount of offering they had given the church, God struck them dead (Acts 5).

The writer of the book of Hebrews explains: "Our fathers disciplined us for a little while as they thought best; but God disciplines us for our good, that we may share in his holiness. No discipline seems pleasant at the time, but painful. Later on, however, it produces a harvest of righteousness and peace for those who have been trained by it" (Hebrews 12:10-11).

In the book of Job, we see another possibility for calamity in our lives—the devil.

One day the angels came before the Lord, and Satan tagged along.

"Where have you come from?" God asked.

"From roaming through the earth and going back and forth in it."

Then God said to Satan, "Did you see my servant Job? There is no one on earth like him; he is blameless and upright, a man who fears God and shuns evil."

"Of course he does," sneered Satan. "Look at all You've done for him. You've blessed the work of his hands, so that his flocks and herds are spread throughout the land. But stretch out Your hand and strike everything he has, and he will surely curse You to Your face" (Job 1:6-11).

God gave Satan permission to strike Job in every possible way, except to take his life. Job lost everything, except his contentious wife, and yet he never knew what (or who) hit him. He never understood why. Through it all, Job did not curse the Lord, but trusted in His sovereign hand.

Oh, how I love the way this story ends. Satan loses. God wins.

Job is blessed. "The LORD made him prosperous again and gave him twice as much as he had before" (Job 42:10).

There is a war going on...a war we cannot see with our eyes but can sense with our spirits. Paul warns us that "our struggle is not against flesh and blood, but against the rulers, against the authorities, against the powers of this dark world and against the spiritual forces of evil in the heavenly realms" (Ephesians 6:12). This war is not fought with hand-to-hand combat, but with spirit-to-spirit prayer. "Your enemy the devil prowls around like a roaring lion looking for someone to devour" (1 Peter 5:8).

Satan is not someone to be feared. James tells us, "Resist the devil, and he will flee from you" (James 4:7). He has no more power over our lives than what we give him.

A third consideration for why tragedy strikes our lives is the fact that we live in a fallen world. There is evil all around us, and sometimes things happen simply because we live in a degenerate society. After the fall of Adam and Eve recorded in Genesis 3, sin entered the world. Do you remember the punishment for anyone who ate of the tree of the knowledge of good and evil? God said they would die. And while Adam and Eve did not immediately die physically, as soon as the forbidden fruit touched their lips, their spirits died.

The Bible tells us, "Sin entered the world through one man, and death through sin, and in this way death came to all men, because all sinned" (Romans 5:12). While most think that the penalty for Adam and Eve's disobedience was being thrown out of the Garden, the real punishment was spiritual death.

Since that time, every man and woman alive has been born with a dead spirit. But God made a provision through His Son, Jesus Christ. Through His death and resurrection, all who believe on Jesus Christ as their Lord and Savior are "born again." They receive a new spirit, a new nature, and a new identity. But we still live in a fallen world.

I like to think of it this way. When we come to Christ, we are saved from the penalty of sin. As we live in this world, we are being transformed from the power of sin. When we leave this world and go to heaven to spend eternity with the Father, we will be saved from the presence of sin. Until then, we live in a fallen world surrounded by the presence of sin.

The Bottom Line

While there is nothing wrong with trying to understand why the wounds of life occur, the Bible clearly tells us not to depend on or lean on our ability to answer the tough question...why? "Trust in the LORD with all your heart," the writer of Proverbs tells us, "and lean not on your own understanding" (Proverbs 3:5). Don't depend on your own mind to figure life out.

Ultimately, God is in control, and His ways are higher than ours. God reminds us, "'For my thoughts are not your thoughts, neither are your ways my ways,' declares the LORD. 'As the heavens are higher than the earth, so are my ways higher than your ways and my thoughts than your thoughts'" (Isaiah 55:8-9). In *When God Doesn't Make Sense,* Dr. James Dobson says, "Trying to analyze His [God's] omnipotence is like an amoeba attempting to comprehend the behavior of man."[1] It's simply not possible.

But there is one thing we can be sure of. "All the ways of the LORD are loving and faithful," whether we understand them or not (Psalm 25:10). "Now we see but a poor reflection as in a mirror; then we shall see face to face. Now I know in part; then I shall know fully, even as I am fully known" (1 Corinthians 13:12). It may not be until we cross over from the temporal to the eternal that we understand the many whys of life. Until then, we must trust in the sovereignty of God.

No matter what we have gone through or what we will go through in the future, God promises: "Do not fear, for I am with you; do not be dismayed, for I am your God. I will strengthen you and help you; I will uphold you with my righteous right hand" (Isaiah 41:10).

God wants to know if we will trust Him no matter what our

outward circumstances may be—even if it means death. Will we say with Job that "though he slay me, yet will I hope in him" (Job 13:15)?

A crisis of belief occurs for most of us during a difficult situation. We know that God, who created the entire universe with but a word, is all-powerful and absolutely able to rescue, heal, or save us—so we tend to feel abandoned or duped when He doesn't. And you can bet your bottom dollar that Satan is going to be waiting in the wings to whisper doubts in your ear. He prowls around like a roaring lion, Peter explains (1 Peter 5:8), looking for just the right moment to discourage the wounded believer.

In the last chapter, we looked at the day Jesus rose from the dead and left the empty tomb. Let's go back to the scene for a moment and join him on the dusty road to Emmaus.

The same day that Peter and John discovered the empty tomb, two of the disciples were walking to the village of Emmaus, about seven miles from Jerusalem. As the sacred city lay behind them, so did their hopes and dreams. While discussing the tragic events of the past weekend, another man appeared and began to walk alongside them.

"What are you talking about?" the man asked.

"Are you the only one visiting Jerusalem and unaware of the things which have happened here in these days?" (Luke 24:18 NASB).

" 'What things?' he asked" (verse 19).

Then the two disciples gave the traveler a blow-by-blow account of Jesus' arrest, crucifixion, and disappearance from the tomb. Their eyes were blinded by despair, and they didn't realize that hope was walking alongside them.

Perhaps you've traveled down your own dusty road to Emmaus, with circumstances leaving you confused, troubled, and depressed. If so, remember this, my friend. Just because we cannot see Jesus or sense His presence does not mean that He is absent. He is walking the path with us. Jesus assures us with these words: "Never will I leave you; never will I forsake you" (Hebrews 13:5). He gave His word. He gave His life.

God is under no obligation to answer our question of why. All through the book of Job, God remained quiet, and then in the last few chapters, He addressed Job's questions.

> Then the LORD answered Job out of the storm. He said: "Who is this that darkens my counsel with words without knowledge? Brace yourself like a man; I will question you, and you shall answer me. Where were you when I laid the earth's foundation? Tell me, if you understand. Who marked off its dimensions? Surely you know! Who stretched a measuring line across it? On what were its footings set, or who laid its cornerstone—while the morning stars sang together and all the angels shouted for joy?" (Job 38:1-7).

God continued to speak to Job. I encourage you to go back and read those magnificent words in Job 38–41 that remind us who God is and who we are not. In the final analysis, Job replied, "I am unworthy—how can I reply to you? I put my hand over my mouth" (Job 40:4).

One of the most beautiful pictures of trusting in the sovereignty of God is in the story of Shadrach, Meshach, and Abednego. These three refused to bow to King Nebuchadnezzar's idol. The punishment for such rebellion against the king was death in a fiery furnace. When the men were taken before the king just before facing death, they respectfully explained:

> The God we serve is able to save us from it [the blazing furnace], and he will rescue us from your hand, O king. But even if he does not, we want you to know, O king, that we will not serve your gods or worship the image of gold you have set up (Daniel 3:17-18).

That is a faith that's real—truly tried by fire. God can deliver me, but if He chooses not to, I'll serve Him anyway. God can heal me, but if he doesn't, I love Him regardless.

By the way, the three men walked out of that furnace without a singed hair on their heads or a hint of smoke on their clothes! And amazingly, as the king watched them walking around in the fire, he noticed not three but four men in the furnace. We can be sure of this: When we are walking through the fiery trials of life, we are not alone. Jesus is right there with us (Isaiah 43:1-2).

Wendy's Crisis of Belief

Wendy grew up in a military family that traveled around the world and never stayed in one place for more than two years. Her family attended church on a regular basis, but they had a religion, not a personal relationship with Jesus Christ. God was someone she read about in a book, but not a heavenly Father she knew personally. Jesus was an icon on a cross, but not a personal Lord.

After high school, Wendy went to Baylor University in Waco, Texas. There she met many wonderful students who exemplified what it meant to be a Christian. And while her interest was piqued, her faith bordered on nonexistent.

It seemed Wendy had everything going for her. Her 5' 7" slender body, long dark hair, and penetrating brown eyes caused people to take notice. Her grades were stellar, her life ordered, and her achievements admirable. By the end of her four years in college, she had an engagement ring on her finger, a job with the university on her calendar, and the promise of law school on the horizon.

But one week after college graduation, Wendy's life took an unexpected turn. One Friday afternoon, she and several of her friends gathered at her apartment complex swimming pool. Being a "sun lover," Wendy was one of the last to leave. She said her good-byes to the friends who lingered by the pool and made her way up the back steps to her apartment. When Wendy came through the back door and walked through the apartment, she noticed that the front door was locked. *I don't remember locking that door,* she thought to herself. A creepy shiver ran up her spine, but Wendy shook it off and proceeded upstairs to her bedroom.

As soon as she rounded the corner, Wendy saw a man standing there. He had a bandana tied around his face with holes cut out for his eyes and wore leather hunting gloves. In his hands he wielded a large, foreboding knife.

At first Wendy thought someone was playing a joke. "What are you doing here?" she asked with a hint of playfulness in her voice. But as soon as one word came out of the man's mouth, Wendy knew that this was no joke.

"Go downstairs and close all the blinds," he ordered. With the knife pointing in her direction, Wendy complied.

"Now, lie on the bed and take your clothes off," he demanded.

"Please don't do this," she begged. "I just got engaged."

"Shut up," he said. "I know all about you and your life."

The man put a wash cloth over Wendy's beautiful face and then proceeded to rape her repeatedly.

"If you tell anyone I did this, I'll come back and kill you," he said as he walked out the door.

After the terrifying ordeal, Wendy went through the horrible aftermath of such an invasion: hospital visits, fingerprint dust through her apartment, the removal of her bed linens for evidence, and repeated telling and retelling of the details.

"I was so confused," Wendy told me. "I always thought that if you lived a good life, then God would be good to you. I didn't drink, smoke, or take drugs. My life was in order, and I had always been a 'good girl.' Why did God let this happen to me?

"I remember being so mad at God," Wendy admitted. "I'd try to go to sleep at night, but I ended up pounding my pillow and crying, 'Why did You let this happen? Why do people love and worship You? I hate You! I hate You!'

"I came to a crisis of belief with three seemingly logical options to pick from. First, God is not all-powerful and, therefore, is unable to protect me. Second, God is all-powerful, but He did not care enough about me to intercede. Finally, God is all-powerful, and He loves me greatly, yet He allowed this to happen to me. That answer scared me the most."

For the next several years, Wendy lived her life in a prison of fear. She wouldn't even take a shower unless someone was in the bathroom with her.

Wendy did get married as planned. She went from counselor to counselor trying to get relief from her trauma. "I was so discouraged," she said. "I would go to rape intervention groups and see women who had been raped ten years prior, and they were still struggling. *Is this how it's going to be?* I wondered."

The frustration, fear, and failure to get relief led Wendy to the *only* place to find true peace—the Bible.

"For the first time, I opened the Bible to explore this God in whom I had always believed but who, in my eyes, had clearly abandoned me," Wendy said. "I wanted answers, so I began to study the Bible to learn that God is sovereign, wise, loving, and holy. I began to see life from God's perspective. He has great purposes in our trials. Trials are not random acts meant to make us miserable or to destroy us. They are meant to refine us and make us strong."

Wendy's journey to freedom is an amazing one—but God's miraculous work in our lives always is. He freed her from the prison of fear and set her on a journey to share the hope that is within her. Through her process of healing, Wendy came face-to-face with Jehovah Rapha—the Healer Himself.

"I am not saying that I am glad the rape happened," Wendy said. "But I see God's hand in the healing process. If that tragedy had not occurred, I would have never set out on this journey to discovering a deep and intimate relationship with God. I would have never had the courage or the passion to minister to other women through counseling in rape support groups, teaching Bible studies, and leading women on their journey to the heart of God. That's the 'good' in Romans 8:28. There is always the 'good.'"

Wendy has found the purpose in her pain. Women are drawn

to her Bible studies because they long to learn about the God who gives her such peace in light of her tragic past.

The Hidden Treasure

So what is the "good" that Wendy mentioned? Romans 8:28 is a verse in the Bible that has been loved and despised by many who mourn. "We know that in all things God works for the good of those who love him, who have been called according to his purpose." What does God mean by "all things"? Most likely it means all things—the good, the bad, and the ugly. God's ultimate goal is not our comfort but our conformity. In every dark circumstance of life, I believe there is a nugget of gold, a hidden treasure, waiting to be discovered. However, for that to happen we must take the dirt, push it aside, and look beneath the surface.

Is it easy? No. Is it messy? Usually. It is worth it? Always.

Many years after we had lost our baby, I was standing in the doorway of Steven's room, observing him in a tangle of sheets and limbs. He was now six feet tall, needed a shave, and sported a mass of shaggy thick brown hair.

"Lord," I prayed, "You know how much I love children and how I always longed to be a mom. Your ways are higher than our ways, and I know that You are my heavenly Father who knows what is best for me, but God, I need a nugget of gold today. I need for You to show me a purpose behind this pain."

Then, God's Word washed over me.

For God so loved the world that he gave his one and only Son, that whoever believes in him shall not perish but have eternal life (John 3:16).

"Is that You, Lord?" I asked.

For God so loved the world that he gave his one and only Son, *that whoever believes in him shall not perish but have eternal life.*

The words refreshed me like a spring rain on parched ground, and for the first time in my life, I truly grasped the height, the depth, and the breadth of those familiar words.

I have a *one and only son*. I love many people in this world, but there is no one…no one…I love enough to sacrifice my only son. And yet God loved me that much. He loved me enough to sacrifice His one and only Son in order to give me life. With tears streaming down my cheeks, I thanked God for helping me understand His great love—for giving me a living, breathing picture indelibly impressed in my mind and on my heart. If that was the only purpose behind the years of infertility and loss of a child, then that was enough.

Joseph Sees the Greater Purpose

Joseph was a man who had many scars in his life. His story is recorded in Genesis 37–50. While he was his father's favorite son, he was his brothers' least favorite sibling. Because their dad, Jacob, showed relentless favoritism toward this child of his beloved wife, Rachel, his brothers were jealous, mocking, and spiteful toward him. Naive Joseph didn't help matters. He flaunted a special ornamented coat that his father had tailor-made just for him, tattled on his brothers for bad behavior, and shared a dream he should have kept to himself.

"Listen to this dream I had," Joseph said to his brothers. "We were binding sheaves of grain out in the field when suddenly my sheaf rose and stood upright, while your sheaves gathered around mine and bowed down to it" (Genesis 37:6-7).

After this revelation, his brothers hated him even more. But the poor boy didn't catch on and told of yet another dream.

"Listen," he said, "I had another dream, and this time the sun and moon and eleven stars were bowing down to me" (Genesis 37:9). This dream was the sheaf that broke the camel's back.

One day his brothers saw an opportunity to get rid of this dreamer once and for all. At first they threw him in a cistern, bloodied his precious coat, and schemed to tell their dad that Joseph had been killed by a wild animal. But while Joseph was still in the pit, deliverance was on the way. Judah noticed a caravan headed to Egypt, and seeing the opportunity to make a bit of profit, the brothers decided to sell Joseph to the slave trader rather than leave him to die. So off he went to a life of slavery.

But the hard times didn't end there. When the slave caravan reached Egypt, Joseph was taken to the home of Potiphar, one of Pharaoh's officials. Potiphar saw that God was with Joseph and he succeeded in everything he did, so Potiphar made Joseph his personal attendant who took care of everything he owned. It seems that Potiphar's wife had her eye on the well-built, handsome young man as well. Several times this desperate housewife tried to coax their new servant into bed, but each time Joseph refused.

Then one day, Joseph went to the house to attend to his duties and none of the household servants were there.

"Come to bed with me," his master's wife begged as she grabbed hold of his cloak.

But Joseph fled, leaving his cloak in the woman's clutched hand. As the saying goes, "Hell hath no fury like a woman scorned." When Potiphar came home, his wife showed him Joseph's cloak and falsely accused him of trying to rape her.

"Look," she said, "that Hebrew slave you bought came to me to make sport of me. But as soon as I screamed for help, he left his cloak beside me and ran out of the house."

The master believed her story and threw young Joseph in prison.

But the hard times didn't end there. While he was in prison, he interpreted the dreams of both the king's former cupbearer and the king's former baker. His only request was, "Remember me when you are released."

The baker was hanged, just as Joseph predicted. And when the cupbearer was released, he forgot Joseph even existed.

Sold into slavery, falsely accused, betrayed, and forgotten. The first 30 years of Joseph's life were filled with more heartache and trouble than most of us would experience in a dozen lifetimes.

But two years later, life took a different turn. Pharaoh had a disturbing dream that no one could interpret. His cupbearer, now restored to his position, then remembered Joseph from his prison days and told the king about his ability to interpret dreams. So Pharaoh sent for the young man.

" 'I cannot do it,' Joseph replied to Pharaoh, 'but God will give Pharaoh the answer he desires' " (Genesis 41:16).

Joseph did indeed interpret Pharaoh's dream, predicted a seven-year famine, and saved the entire Egyptian nation from starvation. As a reward, Joseph was put in charge of the whole land of Egypt. Pharaoh placed his signet ring on Joseph's finger, dressed him in a royal robe, and put a gold chain around his neck. And at age 30, Pharaoh gave Joseph a bride.

Before his thirty-seventh birthday, Joseph had two sons. One he named Manasseh which means "God has made me forget all my trouble and all my father's household" (Genesis 41:51). The second son he named Ephraim which means "God has made me fruitful in the land of my suffering" (Genesis 41:52). Joseph's emotional scars were just as real as the physical ones would have been had he truly been attacked by a wild beast.

Many years passed. During the years of abundance, the Egyptians gathered more grain than they could count. Then when the seven years of famine hit, they had enough grain to sustain their country and the surrounding countries as well. Among those who came to purchase food were none other than Joseph's deceitful brothers. Joseph forged the path of forgiveness and set a standard unmatched until the cross. He was reunited with his family, including his elderly father and younger brother.

Joseph's older brothers were terrified at the punishment they feared would be heaped on their heads. But Joseph saw the hidden treasure in his painful circumstances. "You intended to harm me, but God intended it for good to accomplish what is now being done, the saving of many lives" (Genesis 50:20). Oh, friend, grab onto those words—cling to them. "You intended to harm me but God intended it for good" paves the highway that takes us directly to the destination God had planned all along. He framed his pain in the sovereighty of God.

When Forgetting Is Not Enough

When Joseph learned that his father, Jacob, was ill, he took his two sons, Manasseh and Ephraim, and traveled for one last visit. When they arrived, Jacob said, "Bring the boys to me so I may bless them" (Genesis 48:9).

Joseph brought his sons to his father's bedside. He placed Ephraim on his right toward Jacob's left hand and Manasseh, his firstborn, on his left toward Jacob's right hand. But instead of giving the blessing to Joseph's firstborn, Jacob reached out his right hand and put it on Ephraim's head, though he was the younger, and crossing his arms, he put his left hand on Manasseh's head. Joseph tried to stop his father from giving the blessing to the secondborn rather than the firstborn, but his father refused.

"I know, my son, I know. He too will become a people, and he too will become great. Nevertheless, his younger brother will be greater than he, and his descendants will become a group of nations" (Genesis 48:19). So he put Ephraim ahead of Manasseh.

What a beautiful picture. Yes, Joseph had a life of trouble and suffering at the hands of those who abused, neglected, and betrayed him. But God didn't want him to merely *forget* his suffering as the name Manasseh implied; He wanted him to be *fruitful in his suffering*.

It is the same with you and with me. God does not want us to simply forget the pain of the past. He wants us to be fruitful in the land of our suffering! Use it for good. Minister to others. Plant seeds of hope.

"I will repay you for the years the locusts have eaten...you will have plenty to eat, until you are full, and you will praise the name of the LORD your God, who has worked wonders for you; never again will my people be shamed" (Joel 2:25-26).

Purified as Gold

There are many purposes for the scars of our past. Our understanding of God's character is broadened, our faith is strengthened, our character is matured, our souls are purified, our vision is clarified, our passions are enflamed, and our hearts are softened. Of course, with each of those positive qualities a negative one could occur. For example, our understanding of God could be skewed, our faith weakened, our character compromised, our souls sullied, our vision clouded, our passions extinguished, and our hearts hardened. The sun hardens clay and softens wax; we can either became hard or soft. We can't change our past, but we can determine the effect it will have on our future to make us bitter or better.

I think of all that Job went through: All but three of his servants were murdered, fire from the sky burned up his sheep, the Chaldeans stole his camels, and a mighty wind blew down a house where all his children were feasting...killing them all...and that happened in just one day! (Job 1:13-19).

What did Job do after such losses? He tore his clothes and shaved his head as a sign of mourning. That I can understand. But then we learn: "He fell to the ground in worship..." (verse 20).

Throughout the book of Job we read of more tragedy that befell this one man. Did he question God? Yes. Did he curse God as his wife suggested? No. In the end, after God had spoken to Job, he replied, "My ears had heard of you, but now my eyes have seen you" (Job 42:5). The story of Job is a difficult journey, but what he learned about God was worth the trip! God made him prosperous again and gave him twice as much as he had before. "The Lord blessed the latter part of Job's life more than the first" (Job 42:12).

Whom God Chooses

When God wants to drill a man,
And thrill a man, and skill a man,
When God wants to mold a man,
To play the noblest part;
When He yearns with all His heart
To create so great and bold a man,

> That all the world shall be amazed,
> Watch His methods; watch His ways.
> How He ruthlessly perfects
> When He royally elects!
> How He hammers him and hurts him
> And with mighty blows converts him
> Into trial shapes of clay
> Which only God understands;
> While his tortured heart is crying,
> And He lifts beseeching hands!
> How He bends but never breaks
> When His good He undertakes.
> How He uses whom He chooses
> And with every purpose fuses him;
> But every act induces him
> To try His splendor out—
> God knows what He's about!
>
> HENRY F. LYTE

Jesus Loves Me

It was the first anniversary of the terrorist bombing of September 11, 2001. The rubble from the World Trade Centers had been cleared and the Pentagon repaired, but men and women all across America still mourned the 3000 lives lost on that dark day. In my hometown, a memorial was set up on an expanse of land with a sea of 12-inch white crosses representing the men and women who died.

Kathy and her family went to see the memorial. Along with her 17-year-old daughter, Heather, Kathy took along her three-year-old niece, Taylor. It was difficult for young Taylor to understand exactly what was going on and why so many people were sad, but she obediently walked hand in hand with her cousin between the tiny crosses. At some point, little Taylor wandered away from her family.

The crowd of mourners was reverently silent as they looked at the names inscribed on the white memorials. Some crosses were decorated with flowers, others with teddy bears or other memorabilia. But nothing spoke more poignantly than the silence broken by quiet sobs. Then, as if coming directly from heaven, a small voice could be heard floating on the breeze. Everyone turned to notice a little girl with outstretched arms twirling in circles among the crosses.

With face lifted toward the sky, she sang...

> Jesus loves me, this I know.
> For the Bible tells me so.
> Little ones to Him belong.
> We are weak, but He is strong.
>
> Yes, Jesus loves me.
> Yes, Jesus loves me.
> Yes, Jesus loves me.
> The Bible tells me so.

Time seemed to stand still as hundreds of mourners turned their attention on one small girl with a big message. Even in the midst of pain, even with the loss of life, loss of dreams, and loss of hope... Jesus still loves us. That love can lift the burden of despair, resurrect our dreams, and restore our hope.

Paul reminds us:

> For God, who said, "Let light shine out of darkness," made his light shine in our hearts to give us the light of the knowledge of the glory of God in the face of Christ. But we have this treasure in jars of clay to show that this all-surpassing power is from God and not from us. We are hard pressed on every side, but not crushed; perplexed, but not in despair; persecuted, but not abandoned; struck down, but not destroyed...Therefore we do not lose heart. Though outwardly we are wasting away, yet inwardly we are being renewed day by day. For our light and momentary troubles are achieving for

us an eternal glory that far outweighs them all. So we fix
our eyes not on what is seen, but on what is unseen. For
what is seen is temporary, but what is unseen is eternal
(2 Corinthians 4:6-9; 16-18)

Jesus loves me...this I know.

Scars do not simply represent healing or the end of a struggle,
but the beginning of a ministry! Let's take a look at how God wants
us to use the treasure of our scars to invest in the lives of others.

Four

Redeeming the Pain by Investing in Others

We loved you so much that we were delighted to share with you not only the gospel of God, but our lives as well.
1 Thessalonians 2:8

I had just finished speaking at a women's retreat and decided to settle back and relax as Susie drove me to the airport. "Susie, tell me your story," I said.

"Well, let's see," she began. "My father died when I was four years old. I don't remember much about his illness, but I have missed him ever since. It seems I have looked for him everywhere my whole life. In every man I've ever had a relationship with, it seems I try to find my daddy and the love I know he would have given me had he lived.

"My mother worked from daylight to dark on a farm, trying her best to feed her five children. She worked the fields and fixed the meals, trying to be both a mother and a father. Consequently, I felt like I was robbed of both. I have no memories of her hugging or kissing me or telling me that she loved me. I guess she did, but it was a well-kept secret.

"Because I was poor, I always felt inferior to my peers. I grew up being very shy and insecure."

Susie went on to tell me that she began a search for someone to love her and tell her she was pretty and valuable. She married after her first year of college, and the next 18 years of her life rolled along without much fanfare or incident. But during their eighteenth year of marriage, life began to fall apart. Three of her sisters found out that they had cancer, and her brother got a divorce. Susie began to feel emptiness in her own life, and her husband had no desire to help.

"My husband had his own agenda and couldn't supply the support or the love I so desperately needed," Susie explained. "He even made a game of *not* showing affection. I remember one time I literally chased his car down the street to get a goodbye kiss as he hurriedly rolled up the window. We both laughed, but inwardly I cried. I tried everything to get his attention. I cried, nagged, complained, and even had unnecessary surgeries. Nothing worked."

Susie's husband began to complain that she was pathetic in bed. "Maybe you need to have an affair," he said. "Maybe that will help you!" She was horrified. After all, they were churchgoing people. He was a deacon, and she was a soloist and choir director for the teens.

But the seed was planted and began to take root. Susie decided to have a pool installed in her backyard. When the muscular and tanned construction worker commented on how pretty she was and how good she smelled, Susie drank in those words like parched soil. Susie called her husband on the phone. "Hey, Carl, remember your comment about me having an affair? Were you serious?"

"Sure," he said. "Why? You found someone?"

"I think I have," she said.

"Just be discreet," was his only comment.

Susie did begin an affair with Danny, and later, her husband threatened to kill them both. She loved her husband, but she was addicted to the affection and attention she received from her lover. Susie's husband took away her checkbook, her credit cards, and her home. So she moved out of the house and left her children behind in search of the attention she never found at home.

"Danny was a man who was caught up in Satan's lies, just like me," Susie said. "He gave me more attention and love than I had ever gotten anywhere—as long as I didn't make him mad. When he was angry, be became verbally abusive, telling me I had better be good to him because nobody else would ever want me. I stayed in the relationship for four years."

Susie's promiscuity snowballed after her affair with Danny. She went from man to man searching for love and significance. She married again, but it only lasted for 18 months. Susie got back into church, but she continued her partying lifestyle simultaneously.

Susie married again. "Steve had been more attentive and romantic while dating than any man I had ever known," she explained. "But that came to a screeching halt at the wedding. In fact, the wedding was in the afternoon, and he came home and painted the house, which meant he was too tired to make love at bedtime. He, like me, had been married two other times. Thank God, He got hold of both of us in a church in Florida. Steve became a Christian, and we both became committed to Christ. After a few years, we moved to Texas.

"Sharon, I have asked God to forgive me for everything I did. He has been very good to me. He was there even when I didn't know He was, when I didn't feel He was, and when I didn't even want Him to be. He forgave me and made something good come from the terrible mess I had made. Steve and I have a good life with several grandchildren whom we adore. We are a wonderful example of how God can take a terrible life and make something beautiful from the shattered pieces."

I sat back in my seat. We were now at the airport parking lot sitting in her car. "Susie, how many people in your church know your story?" I asked.

"No one," she replied. "I've never told anyone my entire story."

I was shocked; however, this had happened before.

Because I often share my story, many times women feel safe sharing theirs with me. On many occasions I ask, "How many people know your story?" "No one," most reply.

Like a tightly locked vault, many women hold secrets in their hearts. When God doesn't hold the key, then the enemy does. However, when we realize the power of our scars and redeem the pain by investing in other people, Satan loses all control and the key to the vault slips through his slimy hands.

When I met Susie, she was a bubbly slight woman with short blond hair—the kind of middle-aged woman that all the younger women in her church wanted to emulate. She was on the women's ministry team, sang in the choir, and had an intimate relationship with Jesus Christ. She also had a treasure that she tucked away... her personal story of brokenness and healing.

I wonder how many people Susie could have helped if they had known her story of redemption. I wonder how many young women struggling with the temptation of sexual sin she could have shored up and encouraged if they had known the rocky road she herself had traveled. I wonder how many people would have come to know the Healer Himself, if Susie had had the courage to put the perceived perfect life aside and reveal the truth.

Susie had kept her scars hidden for many years. After our conversation I challenged her to not waste what she had learned, but invest the treasure she had unearthed through the years of dirt. She has agreed to give it a try. We'll come back to Susie in a moment.

A Picture of Redemption

When I was a little girl, my mother did her grocery shopping at White's Supermarket on the corner of Tarboro Street and Pearl.

Other grocery stores were around, but White's gave out S&H Green Stamps with every purchase. On shopping days, I watched as the cashier rang up my mom's purchases, pulling a lever with each entry. My mom's eyes lit up every time she heard the cha-ching, knowing that meant more stamps. When the total tallied, the cash register spit out a stream of stamps, both large and small. We never put the stamps in books right away. Mom stuffed them in a bag and waited until we could make a whole day of it.

About every six months, Mom pulled down a brown paper grocery bag swollen with S&H Green Stamps from a shelf. She spilled its contents on a table and announced, "Okay, Sharon, it's time to paste the stamps."

For hours it was lick, stick, lick, stick, lick, stick. Large stamps represented dollars spent and only three filled a page. Small stamps represented cents spent and 30 filled a page. I liked doing the dollars.

After six months of collecting stamps and six hours of pasting them in the books, my mom and I excitedly drove down to the S&H Green Stamp Redemption Center. With arms heavy laden, we plopped our day's work on the clerk's desk.

"Whatcha gonna get?" I'd ask as we strolled up and down the aisles of housewares.

"I don't know, honey," my mom would reply. "But it'll be something good."

After much consideration, Mom would decide on a treasure such as an electric can opener, a steam iron, or a shiny set of stainless steel mixing bowls. Oh, it was an exciting day to make a trip to the S&H Green Stamp Redemption Center and trade in our stamps for a special prize.

That is a very simple picture of the word "redemption." It means to trade something in for something else, to take my stamps and trade them in (redeem them) for a prize—for something valuable. That's what God can do with our scars if we will trust Him.

"Satan will do everything he can to tempt you not to trust God because he knows your willingness to place yourself in God's holy hands will lead to full redemption...Redemption is when the pain is treated and turned around so thoroughly that it not only loses its power to do you harm but also gains the power to do some good."[1]

The Landowner Returns

Once there was a landowner who decided to go on a long journey. He called three of his servants together and divided up their responsibilities, each according to his own ability. He also entrusted them with a certain amount of money to oversee. The money was weighed out in "talents." To one servant he gave five talents, to one servant he gave two talents, and to the other he gave one talent.

After many months, the master returned and met with the servants to settle their accounts. The servant who had been given five talents had invested the money and doubled his profits—giving the master ten talents. The servant with two talents had invested his money and doubled his as well—giving the master four talents. To both of these the master said, "Well done, good and faithful servant! You have been faithful with a few things; I will put you in charge of many things. Come and share your master's happiness!" (Matthew 25:21).

But then there was the servant with the one talent. He was a fearful and lazy man who didn't want to take a chance. He didn't invest at all, but rather dug a hole in the ground and hid his talent in the dirt. "'Master,' he said, 'I knew that you are a hard man, harvesting where you have not sown and gathering where you have not scattered seed. So I was afraid and went out and hid your talent in the ground. See, here is what belongs to you'" (Matthew 25:24-25).

The master was furious with the fearful servant. He took the one talent and gave it to the one who had ten talents (Matthew 25:28).

I see our scars as priceless treasures that our Master has entrusted to us. We can choose to invest those treasures in the lives of others, or we can choose to hide them because of fear. I have seen how investing the scars from the past in the lives of others has produced dividends far beyond anyone's expectations. One small investment can have resounding effects that continue for generations to come. It is the story of my own life.

Comfort-able

In 2 Corinthians, Paul wrote: "Praise be to the God and Father of our Lord Jesus Christ, the Father of compassion and the God of all *comfort,* who *comforts* us in our troubles, *so that* we can *comfort* those in any trouble with the *comfort* we ourselves have received from God. For just as the sufferings of Christ flow over into our lives, so also through Christ our *comfort* overflows" (2 Corinthians 1:3-5, emphasis added). God does not comfort us simply to make us comfortable. God comforts us to make us comfort-able...able to comfort other people.

A store owner was tacking a sign in his store window that read PUPPIES FOR SALE when a little boy appeared.

"How much are you selling the puppies for?" he asked.

The man told the lad he didn't expect to let any of them go for less than $50.

The boy reached in his pocket, pulled out some change, looked up at the store owner, and said, "I have two dollars and thirty-seven cents. Can I look at them?"

The store owner smiled and whistled. From the kennel, a dog named Lady came running down the aisle, followed by five tiny balls of fur. One puppy lagged behind. Immediately, the little boy asked about the limping puppy.

"What's wrong with that doggie?"

"The veterinarian told us the dog is missing a hip socket," said the store owner. "He'll always limp like that."

"That's the one I want to buy," the lad said quickly.

The store owner replied, "No, you don't want to buy that dog. If you really want him, I'll just give him to you."

The boy came close to the store owner and said angrily, "I don't want you to just give him to me. That doggie is worth just as much as all the other puppies, and I'll pay the full price. In fact, I'll give you two dollars and thirty-seven cents now and fifty cents a month until I have him paid for!"

The store owner replied, "No, no, no. You don't want that dog. He's never going to be able to run and jump and play like the other dogs."

In response, the little boy pulled up his pant leg to reveal a badly twisted left leg, supported by two steel braces.

"Well, sir," he said, "I don't run so well myself and that puppy will need someone who understands."[2]

Dear friend, God may very well send someone your way who needs a person that understands. No one can help a woman who is struggling with a wayward teenager like the mother who has welcomed a prodigal home. No one can encourage a women struggling with depression like the woman who has come out of that same darkness and into the light. No one can help a woman struggling with marital discord like the woman who has seen her marriage transformed from clanging cymbals of contention to a beautiful symphony of love. No one can help a woman struggling with the pain of a shameful past like the woman who has exchanged her tattered sackcloth for a princess's robe.

In *Where Is God When It Hurts?* Philip Yancey notes, "People who are suffering, whether from physical or psychological pain, often feel an oppressive sense of aloneness. They feel abandoned by God and also by others, because they must bear the pain alone and no one else quite understands."[3]

But suppose there is someone who understands? Suppose that person is you or me? Suppose we could be the person to ease the despair of isolation or loneliness because we have been a reluctant traveler down that same road?

Chances are God is going to send someone our way who needs

to hear our stories. Will we open our hearts to reach out to a woman who needs someone who truly understands? Will we expose our scars to give evidence of the healing power of Jesus Christ? Will we invest our lives in other people?

I think the little boy had the right idea.

From the Tombs to the Town

After Jesus had experienced a strenuous day of teaching, not to mention calming a storm, He crossed the Sea of Galilee to enter the region of the Gerasenes. As soon as He stepped off the boat, a demon-possessed man who had been living in the tombs ran up to meet him. This was no welcoming party. The man began to shout at the top of his voice, "What do you want with me, Jesus, Son of the most High God? Swear to God that you won't torture me!" (Mark 5:7).

"What is your name?" Jesus asked.

"Legion," he replied, "because we are many."

You know the saying, "When pigs fly?" Well, this is the day they did. Jesus commanded the demons to come out of the man, and He sent them flying into a nearby herd of swine. Then the entire herd, about 2000 pigs, rushed down the steep bank into the lake and were drowned (Mark 5:9-13).

And what of the man? Before his encounter with Jesus, the tomb-dweller cried out day and night, and cut himself with stones. He even broke the chains that others had used to try and restrain him. But after his encounter with Jesus, the people were amazed to see the previously demon-possessed man sitting fully clothed and in his right mind.

As Jesus was preparing to get in the boat and leave the village, the grateful man ran up to Him, pleading, "Please let me go with you."

But Jesus didn't allow it. Instead, He told him to go back to his family and his village and show his scars.

"Go home to your family and tell them how much the Lord has done for you, and how he has had mercy on you" (Mark 5:19).

Are we surprised? We shouldn't be.

Jesus doesn't comfort us to make us comfortable. He comforts us to make us comfort-able.

Tricia's Investment

Tricia Goyer faced teen pregnancy...twice. It was a scar she would wear for the rest of her life, but would she wear it with guilt and shame or grace and forgiveness? Could God take something that was obviously out of His will, sexual intimacy outside the bonds of marriage, and use it for good? If we believe Romans 8:28, then the answer must be yes. Let's take a moment and let Tricia tell us her story...

"I don't remember the face of the nurse who gave me the news, but I do remember the quiet car ride home with my mom. I remember the first words out of my boyfriend's mouth: 'I don't believe you. It's over, anyway.'

"I was seventeen, pregnant, alone, and I didn't know what to do. It wasn't the first time. Almost two years prior, I'd been dating the same guy and had received the same news. For that pregnancy, I chose the 'easy way out'—only to discover there was nothing easy about the heartache and shame of abortion. There was nothing easy about facing the fact I chose not to carry my child.

"This time I knew having my baby was the right choice. But what about my life? One week I was a cheerleader and an honor roll student. The next week I wasn't. The embarrassment of my expanding waistline compelled me to drop out of school, out of extracurricular activities, out of life. I spent my days sleeping until noon, working on homework for my credits, and watching soap operas.

"When I was six months pregnant, I reached my lowest point. I woke up one day at noon, reaching for the remote control. I was angry my friends didn't call and angry my boyfriend had moved on to someone else. Unexpectedly, I erupted into a torrent of tears, realizing what had become of my life. Yet even as my heart ached, something deep inside told me I didn't have to face this alone. I thought about my Sunday school lessons when I was a little girl. I remembered the joy on my teacher's face as she told me that Jesus loved me. And as I let the words of 'Jesus Loves Me' drift through my mind, I wrapped my arms around my stomach and cried out to God.

" 'Lord, I've messed up. If you can do something better with my life, please do!'

"Tears filled my eyes, and a spark of hope lit my soul. Despite feeling alone, despite concerns of raising a child, even though I felt like a kid myself, I trusted God's plan for my life to be better than the road of self-destruction I was on.

"During the rest of my pregnancy, I occasionally read my Bible and prayed. I tried to live a better life, but I found myself struggling with those same feelings of rejection and isolation. But the day my son was born I began to understand God's faithfulness. Holding my child in my arms filled my heart with love. And for the first time I understood a little more about God's love for me. My son gazed at me with such trust, and I knew I couldn't let him down."

Soon after Tricia returned home with her baby boy, another young man came into her life. John was the son of her pastor and took special interest in the pair. Within the year, they were married. Eight years later, John, Tricia, and their now three Groyer children, moved to Montana to lead a quiet life. They got involved in a wonderful church and made new friends—friends who did not know Tricia's story of teenage pregnancy and abortion.

Let's let Tricia continue…

"My family and friends weren't aware that my inner feelings of unworthiness and rejection were festering like a splinter beneath the skin. I was embarrassed to share the circumstances of my teen pregnancy with my new friends, and I still felt a burden of pain concerning my abortion. More than anything I wanted to leave those things in the past, but how could that happen when the memories of my choices refused to stop haunting me?

"One day at church, a young woman announced a new Bible study class. She said, 'I had an abortion at age nineteen. I've found healing and I want to offer the same hope to others.'

"I was floored! How could she stand in front of the church and share what I couldn't confess to my closest friends?"

It took a month for Tricia to get up the nerve to make the call. On the night of the Bible study, she drove to the church—her heart pounding. But when she entered the class, she discovered other women facing the same issues and the same pain.

As Tricia shared the story of her abortion and subsequent pregnancy, she felt the weight of shame and pain being lifted off her chest. These women understood. She went home clearly aware of God's forgiveness, and she had taken the first step to forgiving herself.

A few weeks later, she felt God prodding her to share her story in church. She stood before the congregation and told her story of pain, shame, and healing. She also expressed the difficulties of being a teenage mother and how it drew her back to God. She was shocked afterward when women—young and old—approached and told her their stories...That is the power of our scars! Tricia soon began reaching out to help those who were burdened by past mistakes, investing in others to help them find forgiveness and hope for the future.

Tricia's Investments Multiply

Tricia continued to mentor women in bondage to past mistakes and failures, but God had an even bigger plan for this young lady. When she was but 27 years old, her pastor approached her about the need for a crisis pregnancy center in their community. At first she panicked, thinking of all the reasons she was not equipped for such a task, but in the end, she chose to obey God's leading. Six months later, Hope Pregnancy Center opened.

"Starting the center took hard work and dedication," Tricia explained. "I not only had to connect with agencies who offered help during crisis pregnancies, but I also had to revisit those past issues I faced as a teenage mother. Yet with every obstacle, God showed us we were on the right path. In less than a year, a local church donated a huge Victorian house for us to use, we were open five days a week, and had forty volunteers. The abortion rate in our community dropped twenty percent."

God continues to open doors for Tricia to invest her scars in others. She initiated a Teen MOPS (Mothers of Preschoolers) group in her community and authored a book for teen mothers titled *Life Interrupted: The Scoop on Being a Young Mom.*

Tricia has experienced the joy of investing her scars in other people. I wonder what her life would be like, and the lives of all those she has touched, had she hidden her treasure in the sand because of fear. I am so thankful she had the courage to make that initial investment and watch it grow exponentially in the lives of so many men and women…not only in her community, but throughout the world.

Gabriel Marcel defines hope as "a memory of the future." That is the gift that Tricia gives every day.

Peter's Challenge to Invest

I'm so glad Jesus picked Peter to be one of His disciples. Time and time again we see him with his foot in his mouth, his pride in his pocket, and his temper on his sleeve. Satan knew Peter was going to have a big impact on the church at large and tried many times to get him off course. During the last supper, Jesus warned Peter that he was about to be tested: "Simon, Simon, Satan has asked to sift you as wheat. But I have prayed for you, Simon, that your faith may not fail. And when you have turned back, *strengthen your brothers*" (Luke 22:31-32, emphasis added).

Peter puffed out his chest, lifted his head, and said, "I am ready to go with you to prison and to death."

I imagine Jesus thought, *Sure you are, son.*

Just a few hours later, the sifting began. As Peter stood by the fire just outside where Jesus was being beaten and tried, a little servant girl asked if he was one of Jesus' followers.

"Woman, I don't know him," he said (Luke 22:57).

Then again...

"Man, I am not [one of his disciples]!" Peter replied (verse 58).

And again...

"Man, I don't know what you're talking about!" (verse 60).

And just as the third denial slipped off Peter's lips, the rooster crowed to remind him of Jesus' words, "Before the rooster crows today, you will disown me three times."

Peter went outside and wept bitterly (verses 61-62).

Jesus knew that Peter was going to deny Him, and yet, before he even fell from grace, Jesus was picking him up. Yes, Peter was absolutely crushed at his weakness in denying Jesus three times. But then the ray of God's love reminded him of Jesus' words: "When you have turned back, strengthen your brothers" (Luke 22:32).

After Jesus' resurrection, He reminded Peter to invest what he had learned in other people. Three times Jesus asked, "Do you love me?" After each of Peter's affirmations, Jesus said, "Feed my lambs...take care of my sheep...feed my sheep" (John 21). Peter did exactly what Jesus asked and spent the rest of his life investing in other people.

Remember Susie, whom we met at the beginning of the chapter? Did she take me up on my challenge not to be ashamed of her scars but find peace and purpose in the pain of her past? Did she follow Peter's lead and take care of God's sheep? Yes, she did. Susie no longer hides her scars under layers of religious perfection. When opportunities arise, she sits side by side with struggling young women and says, "Let me tell you a story."

Like Peter, Susie has learned the joy of redeeming the pain by investing in others.

A Courageous Queen

Katie was born in Wichita, Kansas—a petite blond-headed pride and joy to the Signaigo family. In the following years, two more baby girls were born, and the Signaigo quiver was full. Katie grew up enjoying all the frills and thrills of childhood. She loved school and church activities, swimming and running, and most of all, she loved her friends.

When Katie was nine years old, she noticed a lump by her left ankle that wouldn't go away. The soreness would come and go, but the lump remained. For more than a year, she and her mom were in and out of doctors' offices trying to figure out what this mysterious lump was all about. She was misdiagnosed as having an inflamed tendon, and then again with blood clots.

In desperation and faith, Katie's grandmother and mother laid their hands on the Arkansas phone book and prayed for God to lead them to a doctor that could give them an accurate diagnosis. He did.

In 1991 Katie and her parents walked into a doctor's office at Arkansas Children's Hospital. The doctor took one look at the lump on Katie's ankle and suggested a biopsy. The procedure gave a definitive answer, but it wasn't one they had hoped to hear. Katie had sarcoma...cancer. In less than a week, eleven-year-old Katie lay on an operating room table while the surgeons removed her cancerous leg just below the knee.

"No one will ever love me or want to marry me!" young Katie cried to her mom as they nestled on the hospital bed. "My life will never be the same. What am I going to do? People will laugh at me and make fun of me. I'll never be able to walk or run again. I'm going to have to live the rest of my life in a wheelchair!"

"Oh, precious," her mother spoke in assuring tones, "you will get married one day. You are a beautiful girl. You will run and swim and do all the things you've always loved doing. You are not going to be in a wheelchair, but have a prosthetic leg that will allow you to do all the things you did before. No, your life will not be the same, but it will be great. You'll see. We'll get through this together."

As a precaution, Katie went through chemotherapy for one year. Besides losing her leg, Katie also lost all of her beautiful blond hair. "When is this ever going to end?" she cried.

Young Katie, wise beyond her years, decided that she would just give it all to God. "I know He will take care of me," she said.

Even though she was weak, nauseated, and embarrassed, Katie returned to school.

Eventually, Katie's hair grew back, she learned to walk with a prosthesis, and life returned to normalcy again. However, no one... absolutely no one but her immediate family, saw Katie's leg. She kept her prosthesis hidden from the world.

Katie had become a Christian when she was nine years old, and her relationship with Jesus Christ had continued to grow during those difficult years. When she was 16, Katie felt a nudge from God that it was time for her to redeem the past by investing in others.

"I felt God was nudging me to go back to the children's hospital and talk to other kids who were facing cancer or amputation," Katie explained. "I resisted it. Boy, I resisted it. But one day a nurse called and asked if I could come by for a visit. 'We've got a little girl here who is getting ready to have the same surgery you had six years ago,' she said. 'Could you come and talk to her?'

"So I put my fears aside and made my way up to the cancer ward of the hospital. I showed Amanda my leg and let her touch it. As I talked to her about what I was able to do, I could actually see something in her eyes. It was hope."

From that time on, Katie and her mom have made many visits to the hospital, telling children and their parents about what to expect and sharing hope. Together they are taking their scars, both physical and emotional, and investing in others.

But the story doesn't end there. Katie graduated from high school and attended the University of Central Arkansas. While there, she watched an Oprah program that featured Aimee Mullins, a double amputee who had become an athlete and a model.

Aimee spoke freely about her amputations and her prosthetic legs. She even showed various legs she used for different occasions.

Watching Aimee gave Katie the courage to not be ashamed of her prosthetic leg. "Because of Aimee's confidence and comfort with herself, I was able to start to fully accept myself," Katie explained.

With newfound confidence, Katie decided to make her debut in a grand way. Katie entered the Miss UCA (University of Central Arkansas) pageant. Katie seemed like any other contestant as she participated in the talent, evening gown, and interview competitions. But she won the hearts of the crowd when she proudly walked down the catwalk...in the bathing suit competition. There have been many tearful moments as pageant sponsors have placed the crown on a winner's head. But, I daresay, there was never a more precious moment than when Katie Signaigo was crowned Miss University of Central Arkansas. Katie went on to compete in the Miss Arkansas pageant some months later.

After Katie won the crown, she wrote Oprah Winfrey to thank her for airing the inspiring program that had encouraged her to not be ashamed of her prosthetic leg. She also told Oprah about her courageous move to participate in a pageant and the resulting win.

A few days later, Katie's phone rang.

"Hello, is this Katie Signaigo?"

"Yes, it is."

"Hi, Katie," the woman continued. "I am calling from the Oprah Winfrey program. We received your letter and would like to have you as a guest on the show."

The next day, a film crew from Chicago showed up at Katie's door. They taped her talking to patients at the hospital and interacting with her family. Then they whisked her off to the *Oprah* show, where Katie talked about finding peace and purpose in her amputation and recovery.

Katie is now 24 years old and teaching music to high school students. But her first love is telling about Jesus Christ and sharing the peace and hope that only He can give. She has faced more trials than most people twice her age, and loves helping those who are traveling down the road of uncertainty called cancer.

"We are all cracked pots in some way or other," Katie told a group of ladies at a women's gathering. "We all have our unique flaws. Don't be afraid of your flaws. Look for the positive things in life. Don't let yourself dwell in the bad things. This has been the greatest blessing in my life."

Katie has learned the joy of redeeming the pain by investing in others. And I have a feeling that this is just the beginning for her.

FIVE

Replacing the Wounds with Scars

Do you want to get well?
JOHN 5:6

Barbara's face bore the lines and creases of a woman dragging around years of bitterness and regret. After hearing my story, she asked if we could talk for a while. We sank into an overstuffed couch, and she began.

"I was raised in a 'religious' home, the youngest of twelve children," she explained. "My father drank very heavily and continually belittled all of us. My mom did very little to protect us, even when he made us girls parade around in our underwear. I think she was afraid of him. He always cut her down, and she seemed nervous most of the time.

"My dad told us that the first four kids were planned," she

65

continued. "But the rest of us were accidents. I was one of the accidents.

"All of us kids used to take baths together, and I remember one of my brothers touching me inappropriately. Several years later, I remember touching one of my neighbors in a similar way.

"I hear what you say about 'letting go of the past,'" she continued, "and that 'God forgives us when we ask.' I know that the Bible says 'we are a new creation in Christ, the old is gone, the new has come,' but I just can't forgive myself for what I've done and I can't forgive my father for making me this way. I can't let go!"

Barbara and I talked for a very long time, and I could see we were getting nowhere. Finally, I said, "Barbara, let's pray."

Please hear me. I don't want you to think that this is harsh, but God revealed something to me during that prayer time. It wasn't that Barbara *couldn't* let go of the past. It was that she *wouldn't* let go of the past. Like a child who continues to pick at a scab, Barbara continued to pick at the scabs of her life, never giving them a chance to heal.

Forgetting What Lies Behind

There is much of my childhood that I do not remember. I have a vague memory of two or three incidents from birth to six years old. I have only a few memories of when I was seven, and not until I was eight do memories start appearing clearly on the screen. The few memories I do have from my early years are not pleasant. I remember my father hitting my mother, throwing things in the house, and violent arguments. I recall tense meal times, horrific holidays, and lonely, unattended school events. I recall hiding in a dark closet or retreating to the roof and letting my imagination take me to a place where I was loved and cherished, but traumatic events have a way of casting a dark cloud over the sunny days. There were happy times too. I warmly recall my mom cooking wonderful Southern meals—chicken-and-dumplins being my favorite. I remember summers at my grandmother's house and always feeling as though I were her favorite (I'm sure all of her grandchildren felt that way.) I also remember vacations at the beach where my love affair with the shore began. Yes, there were happy times.

As I grew older, certain memories began to surface, I began to understand the source of many of my insecurities. It was only when I began to understand them that I was able to heal. Scientists have shown that men remember events, and women remember not only events, but the emotions attached to them. It's the emotions that keep us from healing.

As humans, we tend to remember what we need to forget and forget what we need to remember. God, on the other hand, forgets what He promises to forget and remembers what He promises to remember. God said, "Their sins and lawless acts I will remember no more" (Hebrews 10:17).

Paul tells us one of the secrets to his success as a Christian and in life. "One thing I do: Forgetting what is behind and straining toward what is ahead, I press on toward the goal to win the prize for which God has called me heavenward in Christ Jesus" (Philippians 3:13-14).

But wait, doesn't that contradict the message of this book? How can we "forget what is behind" and discover the beauty of our scars at the same time? The key lies in a biblical understanding of the word "forget."

In the Bible, God tells us that He "forgets" our sins and remembers them no more. But how does an omnipotent, all-knowing God *forget?* Let's look at the antonym to get a better understanding.

There are many events in the Bible that begin with the words "God remembered": "God remembered Noah" (Genesis 8:1), "he (God) remembered Abraham" (Genesis 19:29), "God remembered Rachel" (Genesis 30:22), "God heard their groaning and remembered his covenant with Abraham, with Isaac and with Jacob" (Exodus 2:24). In each incident, God remembering meant that He was about to do something—God was about to act.

Therefore, if God *remembering* means He is about to act, then

God *forgetting* means that He is *not* going to act. "For I will forgive their wickedness," He says, "and will remember their sins no more" (Jeremiah 31:34). He forgets our sins—He is *not* going to act upon them. Likewise, while we cannot physically forget the details of the wounds of our pasts, we can choose to not act on them. We can choose to forgive the person who has hurt us and not allow the memory of the offense to control our lives. In that sense, we can forgive and forget.

When Paul talks about forgetting, he does not mean that he will or even can wipe an incident from his memory. "Forgetting did not mean obliterating the memory of his past, but was a conscious refusal to let it absorb his attention and impede his progress."[1] Paul refused to allow anything from his past control his present. He could tell about it, but without pain, malice, or a hint of revenge.

Yes, I do remember the wounds from my past, but I can honestly say I no longer act on them. When I remember, I do not feel the sting, taste the bitterness, or hear the ringing of injustice. My past no longer controls my present. Because the memories have so little power over my actions and emotions these days, they come to the surface much less often. Satan has had to dig into his bag of tricks for a different type of ammunition because his old tricks of the fiery darts of the past simply aren't effective. To me, that's forgetting the past.

But it's too hard, you might say. Friend, God will never tell us to do something that He will not give us the power to do. He has instructed us to forgive...so He will give us the power to do so. He has instructed us to leave the past behind...so He will give us the power to do so. He has instructed us to put off the old self...so He will give us the power to do so. Paul said, "I can do all things through Christ who strengthens me" (Philippians 4:13 NKJV). "All things" means all the things God has called us to do.

Isaiah wrote, "When a farmer plows for planting, does he plow continually? Does he keep on breaking up and harrowing the soil? When he has leveled the surface, does he not sow caraway and scatter cummin? Does he not plant wheat in its place, barley in its plot, and spelt in its field?" (Isaiah 28:24-25).

I think for many of us, we have been plowing and replowing the ground far too long. We've been telling and retelling what was done and how it was done...going over the same ground and stirring up the dirt into a giant dust bowl. But there comes a point when it is time to stop plowing up the ground and start planting seeds—until then, we will never see a harvest.

Do You Want to Get Well?

Sometimes the chains we wear shackled to our hearts become so comfortable, we get used to the pain and forget what it is like to be well. Perhaps some of us have never known freedom. But the big question is—do you *want* to get well? Do you *want* to be free? *Of course I do,* I hear you say. But do you *really?*

There was a certain man Jesus encountered who faced the same crossroads in his life. In Jerusalem, men and women with various infirmities congregated at the Sheep Gate Pool. Surrounding the pool were five porticoes where sick people clustered, waiting for the "moving of the waters." They believed an angel of the Lord came down from heaven at certain seasons and stirred the pool. When the people saw the waters ripple, they all made a mad dash to jump in. They believed that the first one to make it to the pool would be healed.

One man, an invalid, had been waiting by the pool for 38 years. When Jesus saw the man lying there and learned that he had been doing so for such a long time, he asked him, "Do you want to get well?" (John 5:6).

That seems like an unusual question—or does it? Sometimes we become accustomed to being "sick." We become attached to our wounds. They become a part of who we are, and we can't imagine life without them. For this man, healing meant a drastic life change. He would have to get a job, become a responsible adult, and stop lounging by the pool all day.

Pain can become an idol. Not that we worship it in a good

sense, but we worship it as an awesome force and allow it to control our lives. When we allow our past to dictate our future, we are giving it the power of a god and making it an idol. "We can hug our hurts and make a shrine out of our sorrows or we can offer them to God as a sacrifice of praise. The choice is ours."[2]

Did the invalid want to get well? He had not asked for Jesus' help. It seems he clung to his illness and blamed it on those around him—a victim of circumstance. "I have no one to help me into the pool when the water is stirred" (John 5:7). We don't know if he had lost the will to be healed, was afraid to lose the income of a beggar, or simply had accepted lameness as his lot in life. In any case, unexpectedly he came face-to-face with the One who could set him free.

The man never did answer Jesus' question. Jesus simply said, "Get up! Pick up your mat and walk" (John 5:8). And he did.

Thirty-eight years is a long time to be immobile, and yet, in my own life, there were some things that had held me back for the same amount of time. I was paralyzed by feelings of inferiority, insecurity, and inadequacy because of messages from my past. Then Jesus asked me, "Do you want to get well?"

Satan wants to use our past to paralyze us. God wants to use our past to propel us. The choice is ours.

A Helping Hand

Can I take you to another man who was lame? Oh, how this story in Mark 2:1-12 stirs my heart!

One day Jesus traveled to Capernaum, Peter's hometown. The people there had heard about how Jesus healed the sick, made the lame to walk, and cast out evil spirits. That evening people crowded into every nook and cranny of Peter's home, even overflowing out the door, to hear Jesus.

But Jesus' voice was not the only thing heard among the crowd. Hammering. Pounding. Digging. Scraping. After a short time, Jesus noticed that clay from the ceiling was beginning to rain down on

His head and sprinkle His lashes. Dust piled up around His sandaled feet and powdered His cloak. As Jesus raised His eyes to the ceiling, He discovered a growing opening and four very determined men.

After quite some time, the crowd stared wide-eyed as a man was lowered through the opening on a mat and placed at Jesus' feet. Jesus looked down at the paralyzed man lying on the pallet before him and simply said, "Your sins are forgiven" (Mark 2:5).

But wait. Is that what the man really longed for? Is that what his friends had in mind? Oh, my friend, sometimes it *is* our sin that paralyzes us. One of Satan's most damaging tactics is to paralyze us with our own emotions. He wants to cover us with shame, weigh us down with guilt, and cripple our progress toward the cross. But Jesus came to set us free! He tells us to get up and walk!

There is another facet of this story that sets my heart to singing. The man's friends loved him enough to carry him to Jesus. Sometimes we don't have the energy to make it to the Healer alone. How blessed to have friends who will be the stretcher bearers to carry us to the Savior, risk the rebuke of others, and are not afraid of getting a bit messy in the process.

Psychologists say that it is difficult for a person to maintain mental health unless he has at least one person with whom he can be completely emotionally honest.[3] Jesus had 12 close friends, and three best friends—Peter, James, and John. It is a gift to have one person with whom we can be completely honest. How much better if we can have two or three.

Someone once said, "A friend hears the song in my heart and sings it to me when my memory fails." A friend can remind me of God's faithfulness when my memory is clouded by the circumstances of life.

- Do you have a friend who is emotionally or spiritually paralyzed because of the sins or trauma of her past? How far are you willing to go to help her?

- Are you emotionally or spiritually paralyzed because of the sins or trauma of your past? Are you willing to let someone help you walk again?

James tells us, "Humble yourselves before the Lord, and he will lift you up" (James 4:10). He won't necessarily lift you up to a place of worldly honor, but He will lift you up out of the dirt, off the mat, and set your feet on the path He has chosen for you all along. Sometimes He might call a friend to be your stretcher bearer. Other times He might call you to be that friend for someone else.

Healing Is a Process

Healing is a process. We don't know much about what happened after those two lame men were healed, but I imagine they each had to learn how to stand on their own two feet—literally and figuratively.

Healing begins by recognizing that a wound needs to be healed— a painful memory, a festering bitterness, an aching heart. Healing usually doesn't happen in an instant, but through a process of steps or decisions. Webster defines "process" as "a series of acts or changes, proceeding from one to the next, a method of manufacturing or conditioning something, a moving forward, especially as part of a progression or development."[4]

One of my favorite words in the New Testament is "immediately." "Immediately they received their sight" (Matthew 20:24), "immediately the leprosy left him" (Mark 1:42), "immediately her bleeding stopped" (Luke 8:44). Sometimes God heals...*immediately.* Sometimes He chooses to send us through a process of healing steps. Either way, I have learned that He is more concerned with the process than the finished product. Of course, I prefer the "immediately" route, but most of the time it seems I travel through the valleys and mountain ranges as did Much Afraid in the classic book *Hinds Feet on High Places.*

The good news is that Jesus never encountered someone whose infirmity was greater than His power to heal it. You might think that you are too far gone. Rest assured, Jesus specializes in bringing life from death, no matter how long death has prevailed.

In the Bible there are three incidents of Jesus' raising someone from the dead: the widow of Nain's son (Luke 7:11-17), Jairus' daughter (Luke 8:41-56), and Lazarus, brother of Mary and Martha (John 11:1-57). Jairus' daughter had been dead only a few hours, the widow of Nain's son had probably been dead a few days, and Lazarus had been dead long enough for his body to begin to decay. Neither the length of time the person had been dead nor the amount of deterioration that had taken place mattered to Jesus. One word from Him, and they were back on their feet!

Likewise, no matter how long we have felt the pain from a seemingly fatal wound of the soul, God can restore and resurrect our broken dreams. He can even create a vast army from a pile of dried up bones. He told the prophet Ezekiel to speak to a hovel of bones.

> Prophesy to these bones and say to them, "Dry bones, hear the word of the LORD! This is what the Sovereign LORD says to these bones: I will make breath enter you, and you will come to life. I will attach tendons to you and make flesh come upon you and cover you with skin; I will put breath in you, and you will come to life. Then you will know that I am the LORD..." So I prophesied as he commanded me, and breath entered them; they came to life and stood up on their feet—a vast army. (Ezekiel 37:4-6,10).

If God can take a pile of old dry bones and change them into a vast army, then He can certainly take the broken pieces of our lives and transform us into mighty warriors for Him. Eric Liddell once said, "Circumstances may appear to wreck our lives and God's plans, but God is not helpless among the ruins."

Grieving the Loss

Beth is one of my dearest friends. She had been married for 24 years when her husband walked away from their marriage. Beth is a very strong Christian, and for five years put on a happy face, telling everyone, including herself, "Jesus is enough." She has two absolutely incredible children who love the Lord and both serve in some facet of ministry. And yet, I wondered if she had been the first person I had ever known who had skipped the grieving process that follows the devastation of divorce.

She was not.

Five years after the divorce, Beth and I were talking on the phone about the wonderful man that she had been dating for two years.

"Beth, what's wrong with Randy? Why is he dragging his heels?" I asked. "I'm ready to hear some wedding bells."

"Sharon," she replied, "I don't think the problem is Randy. I think it's me. I was married for twenty-four years and, honestly, I am having trouble trusting again. I know Randy is not anything like my first husband. He loved his wife and they had an incredibly Christ-centered marriage before she died of cancer. But there's just something wrong with me!"

"Beth, I don't think you ever allowed yourself to grieve over your loss. I know your first husband betrayed you at the very core of what a marriage is supposed to be, but there is still a loss. There is grieving the loss that your children do not have the father they deserve, the loss of investing twenty-four years in a man who betrayed you, and the loss of the dream of what marriage could and should be like—what God intended from the beginning of time."

Beth is just now beginning to grieve the many losses that accompanied her divorce and she—and her two grown children—are in the process of breaking free.

In *On Death and Dying,* Elisabeth Kubler-Ross notes five stages of grief:

- Stage One: Denial and Isolation
- Stage Two: Anger

- Stage Three: Bargaining
- Stage Four: Depression
- Stage Five: Acceptance

But for us who have linked our lives with Jesus Christ, there is a Stage Six:

- Resurrection

Grief is part of the healing process. For me, I had to grieve the fact that I did not have the family I had always longed for. I grieved that I did not grow up being the apple of my daddy's eye, that I was not unconditionally loved, and that I did not get to hold my second child in my arms. Grieving each loss helped me to let it go. But after a time, I had to stop lamenting what was not and rejoice in the blessings of what is. Remember, you can't change the past, but you can change what you choose to do with it.

Perhaps you need to grieve for losses in your life. Here are a few:

- Loss of innocence
- Loss of a nurturing family
- Loss of unconditional love
- Loss of acceptance
- Loss of security
- Loss of virginity
- Loss of a close relationship with your mother
- Loss of a healthy relationship with your father
- Loss of trust
- Loss of education
- Loss of employment
- Loss of a marriage

- Loss of a spouse
- Loss of a child
- Loss of friendship

It is healthy to grieve a loss, but then there comes a time for the mourning to end and new life to begin.

> My lover spoke and said to me,
> "Arise, my darling,
> my beautiful one, and come with me.
> See! The winter is past;
> the rains are over and gone.
> Flowers appear on the earth;
> the season of singing has come,
> the cooing of the doves
> is heard in our land."
> SONG OF SONGS 2:10-12

Living in Freedom

When I was in the twelfth grade, we had to do a term paper. For some strange reason, I did my research project on "The Recidivism Rate of Prison Inmates." I know, I know. Why? For the life of me I can't remember. But I did learn a few interesting facts about how often prison inmates who served their time and were set free returned to prison again.

Let me give you some updated statistics. Among 300,000 prisoners released in 15 states in 1994, 67.5 percent were rearrested for a new offense within three years. Forty-nine percent were reconvicted for a new crime. Nearly 52 percent (51.8) were back in prison serving time for a new prison sentence or a technical violation of their release, such as failing a drug test, missing an appointment with their parole officer, or being arrested for a new crime.[5]

For some, being in prison is more comfortable than being on

the outside. They know how to function in prison, and being on the outside, living in freedom, is too foreign, too difficult, or too complicated. A life of bondage is easier.

Sometimes wounded people grow so comfortable with their wound they become unsure how to live without it. It becomes who they are, and they are afraid of the free world. Prison bars create a sense of security. At least they know what to expect, and very little is required of them.

But Jesus came to set the captive free and to give abundant life.

So the question remains, *Do you want to get well?*

Moving Past the Pain

I sat by the bedside of a 55-year-old friend, listening to him rehearse all his past injustices yet again. Stan was relatively healthy, but he had a scare from a tumor that showed up on a chest X-ray. The growth proved to be benign, but the healing of the incision would take several months. While the surgeon had expertly excised the ganglion mass, the cancerous mass in his soul still remained.

During our visit, Stan played and replayed his footage of childhood hurts, going from scene to scene as though he were a movie critic pointing out the weakness and foibles of the actors on the set. Like an old black-and-white movie marred by static and time-worn film, I listened to his perception of the past and how it continued to affect him today.

Everything in me wanted to scream, "Enough!" I wanted to grab the invisible crutch that had become his excuse for poor behavior and break it over his stubborn head.

"How are you any different from the father you despised?" I wanted to ask.

Of course I didn't. I just listened...again.

What would Jesus say to Stan? What has Jesus most likely asked before?

"Stan, do you want to get well?"

We each have a choice when it comes to replacing our wounds with scars. I'll admit, it can be frightening—especially if the wound is all we've ever known. Like a fledgling unsure of its ability to navigate the vastness of the open skies, we perch on the edge of the nest, wondering if we could survive outside its safe boundaries. Something inside us tells us that we were not made for the nest, but will we venture beyond and take flight?

Oh, my friend, I hope your answer is yes!

In the next two chapters, we'll look at two necessary steps in replacing the wounds with beautiful scars—forgiving those who have hurt us and forgiving ourselves. So take a deep breath. This could be the most treacherous mountain to climb on the journey, but the view from the top will take your breath away.

SIX

Restoring the Broken Heart

*The Spirit of the Sovereign LORD is on me,
because the LORD has anointed me to preach good news
to the poor. He has sent me to bind up the brokenhearted,
to proclaim freedom for the captives and release from darkness
for the prisoners...to comfort all who mourn.*
ISAIAH 61:1-2

"What I really wanted was to climb up in my mother's lap and be held, but instead she yelled, 'Get out of my sight! I can't stand to look at you. If it weren't for you, I wouldn't have so many problems.' So I crept down the hall and out of sight. Hungry and afraid, I wanted to go where I wouldn't be a problem for anyone...sometimes I wanted to die."

Mary came into the world an unwanted, unloved child. In an

effort to abandon her eighth child, Mary's mother escaped the hospital and left her newborn baby in the nursery, hoping someone else would take her home. However, the authorities located Mary's mother and issued a court order for her to take her daughter home. Thus began Mary's journey in a cold, cruel, and lonely world.

"All I ever wanted was to climb up in my mother's lap and be lovingly embraced," Mary explained. "But what I got were words such as 'I can't stand to look at you.' 'Get out of my sight.' 'You're just another mouth to feed.'

"There were many days I just wanted to disappear. I knew no one would miss me, not even my brothers and sisters, and certainly not my mother. She constantly yelled at me to 'stay out of her sight.' I was more trouble than the rest of the kids because I was so young."

Mary's mother often exiled her to a rock garden in the backyard. Even though she had seen snakes in the area, her mother continued to send her to the same spot day after day.

"I so desperately wanted to run and hide," Mary remembered, "or at least find a safe place with someone who would love me. But I could not think of one single person who would be glad to see me. I spent many days hungry and thirsty. I wondered if God had any use for a little girl like me. No one ever said I was good for anything; rather, I was always in the way. My sisters used to tell my mother I did things I didn't do just so I would be punished and kept out of their way."

Much of Mary's early life was but a whisper of a memory, but one incident would haunt her for many years to come. When she was six year old, the very year her father died, a man came into their lives. He told her he was her uncle, but she knew he wasn't. He brought her presents, showered her with attention, and seemed to enjoy spending time with the family. It wasn't long until he zeroed in on the littlest member of the family who was also the loneliest and most vulnerable—Mary. When he offered to take little Mary over to his house to look after her, her mother was only too quick to consent. The man began to touch Mary in private places, and over time the sexual abuse escalated to more than touching. She prayed that the man would leave her alone, but he continued to come to take little Mary to his house.

"Home is a place where a child should feel safe," Mary said. "But this man had seen my loneliness and befriended me. He systematically coaxed me to trust him. To most, I appeared to be the same. I went to school, talked to neighbors, and played in the yard, but what I was letting this man do to me sent me to an abyss of despair.

"I so wanted to tell someone of the abuse, but he threatened to throw me into the river or into a pit of snakes if I breathed a word. I was six. I believed him. I knew it was wrong, but I didn't know how to stop him."

So at six years old, Mary felt her life was over. She saw herself as a dirty little girl living a life of ugliness...she felt worthless, lost, and alone. She learned how to lie and put on a mask to hide her pain. She walked and talked and slept, but many times she simply pretended to be someone else. Mary became painfully shy and introverted, never allowing others to see past the facade.

"Every time I saw a little girl who looked pretty, I wanted to be her," Mary explained. "Every time the teacher raved about another child, I tried to copy what that child did. I worked very hard to please others, but it didn't seem to make much difference. I fantasized about someone coming into my life and taking me home to be their little girl. I longed for someone who would love me and be happy to have me as their own. I needed love, but I couldn't seem to find anyone to give it. In seeking approval, I was playing a game that I knew I could never win."

The sexual abuse continued for three years. Somehow, at age nine, Mary mustered up enough courage to tell this man that if he ever touched her again, she would tell. Mary had no idea *who* she would tell, but the threat worked and the man never touched her again.

The sexual abuse was just one facet of Mary's painful childhood. Her mother was a "rageaholic" with almost nightly outbursts of anger. Many times she flew into rages and broke all the dishes in the house or tore all their clothes to shreds.

Along the way there were glimpses of another life. One neighbor often felt sorry for her and brought her cookies. A social worker who discovered that she was left alone for hours at a time took her on house visits and gave her crayons and a coloring book. A couple who saw her dressed in a threadbare dress ringing the Salvation Army bell at Christmas bought her a beautiful blue sweater. A teacher, Mrs. Foster, took special interest in her and picked her for a part in a school play.

"Mrs. Foster was happy all the time, and she was always glad to see me," Mary remembered. "She didn't make fun of my shabby clothes or my messy hair. She told me I was smart and could read well. She even picked me to be part of a school play. I was a tree, but I was the best tree ever! I knew how to stand very still and be very quiet. Mrs. Foster helped me reclaim some pride and dignity. She heard about how my mother always belittled me, and we seemed to have a silent pact. She saw the necessity of making my mother think I was a very good little girl. For the first time someone was nice to me and didn't want anything in return. I could just be a little girl—dirty and unclean, but clearly cared for and loved by this teacher."

Yes, God sent glimpses of sunlight into this dark little life. And Mary caught a ray of hope that one day, things would be better.

Scars of an Unwanted Child

The wound of being unwanted or feeling unwanted as a child is one of the most difficult to heal. While Mary faced many difficulties in her life: sexual molestation, a mentally unstable mother, poverty, hunger, neglect, alcoholic parents and siblings, and later a brain tumor and breast cancer, the wound that went deeper than any other was being unwanted and unloved by her mother.

Why is that such a difficult obstacle to overcome? I believe it is because it goes against the very nature of what God intended in a relationship between a mother and her child. Our bodies are designed to nurture with breasts to suckle a newborn, hips to balance a toddler, and a heart to cherish for a lifetime. Rejection from a parent hits at a child's core need to be loved.

In *Silver Boxes,* Florence Littauer compares encouraging words to silver gift boxes with bows on top. All day long we give, receive, and sometimes steal silver boxes from others. "When it is a mom who steals our box," Florence explains, "we can end up feeling like plain brown wrapping paper looking for the glow of the silver paper for the rest of our lives."[1]

No parent is perfect. None of us can be available all the time—physically or emotionally. From time to time we are too controlling, too protective, or too permissive. We lose our temper, our patience, and our control. We fly off the handle and we fly by the seat of our pants. We have feet of clay—we're human. But all in all, most kids know their parents love them...don't they?

If you ask kids, you might be surprised.

Most kids can handle an occasional outburst of anger if they have plenty of love deposited in their emotional bank accounts. But if anger and rejection are constant, that child will be emotionally bankrupt. Unfortunately, many never recover.

When a seed of rejection is planted in a child's heart, it continues to grow as the child grows. The end result is an adult who feels worthless, useless, and unlovable. Every thought or message is interpreted through a sieve of inferiority, inadequacy, and insecurity. It is easy to describe the pain of being physically or verbally abused, but it can be difficult to describe the pain of being physically or emotionally neglected. "Sins of omission" we call them. What was not done, rather than what was done.

Many times the parent who withholds affection or love comes across as a victim of ill circumstances. Therefore, the child or the adult child feels guilty for the wounds and does his or her best to ignore them or cover them up.

In *Toxic Parents,* Dr. Susan Forward notes,

Whether it's "they didn't mean to do any harm," or "they did the best they could," these apologies obscure the fact that these parents abdicated their responsibilities to their children. Through this abdication, these toxic parents robbed their children of positive role models, without which healthy emotional development is extremely difficult."

If you are the adult child of a deficient or inadequate parent, you probably grew up without realizing that there was an alternative to feeling responsible for them. Dancing at the end of their emotional string seemed a way of life, not a choice.[2]

Did you notice in Mary's story that she felt that her mother's rage was somehow her fault? One reason is because her mother plainly told her it was. A three-year-old can't reason and come to the conclusion "Now, I know I'm not bad. There's no way I can be the cause of all my mother's problems. Look at her. She has eight kids, no husband, and no skills. She is mentally unstable, drinks too much, and has no control over her emotions. I'm not bad. My mom is just sick."

A child can't reason as an adult, but rather tends to blame himself or herself for neglect and abuse. The alternative is too painful. Home is supposed to be your safe place. Parents are supposed to be your protectors. It is easier for children to feel guilt than to admit the very foundations of their lives are missing.

Maybe the wounds you face from childhood are not like Mary's, but you know they are there. Remember this: "You are not responsible for what was done to you as a defenseless child. You *are* responsible for taking positive steps to do something about it now."[3]

Can I say that again? You are not responsible for what happened to you as a child. You were a child! The responsibility comes when we decide what we are going to do with the wound. Pick at the scab or allow it to heal into a beautiful scar.

Ignored by Man, Chosen by God

I was struck by the scenario of when the prophet Samuel went to anoint the next king of Israel. By God's instruction, Samuel went to Bethlehem to the house of Jesse. He knew where to go and what family the king would come from. He knew the next king would be one of Jesse's sons...he just didn't know which son.

Samuel arrived in Bethlehem and asked Jesse to bring all of his sons out for his inspection. Jesse brought out each of his seven sons one by one. As Samuel prayerfully approached each young man, God said, "No, that is not the one...No, that is not the one...No, that is not the one." Seven times God refused Jesse's sons. Finally, exasperated and confused, Samuel asked, "Are these all the sons you have?" (1 Samuel 16:11).

"Oh yeah, I do have one more son," Jesse said. "I almost forgot all about him. Little David is out taking care of the sheep. I'll send someone to get him."

David was so insignificant to his own father that when the prophet requested an audience with *all* of his boys, the dad didn't even think to invite him. However, he was the very one God had selected to be the next ruler of His chosen people. How exciting! You may have felt overlooked, disregarded, and ignored by your earthly family, but God has chosen you to be His child!

Sexual Abuse

In addition to the verbal abuse and sense of abandonment, Mary also suffered sexual abuse from a family friend. Sexual abuse is a horrific invasion of a child's heart and soul, because the very person or persons whom the child is supposed to look to for protection is the person from whom he or she needs to be protected.

A key component of sexual abuse is the "secret factor." Perpetrators always threaten the child in order to keep him or her quiet. Emotional blackmail may include "If you tell, I'll kill your mother," "If you tell, I'll kill you," and "If you tell, no one will believe you." It is a dirty little secret, and most of the time the child is so ashamed he or she is willing to remain silent. Shame is the underlying current that courses through the veins of a child who has been sexually abused. And the river does not stop simply because the child becomes an adult or because the abuse has come to an end. It continues to silently flow like hidden sewage pipes under the streets of a busy city.

Some sins we can toss away like old garbage. But the problem with sexual sin or sexual abuse is that we carry it around in our bodies. There's just no getting away from it.

If the sexual abuse is by a family member, which in most cases it is, the child may keep quiet for fear of breaking up the family. Most children long for a cohesive family unit, no matter how dysfunctional that unit may be.

Dr. Susan Forward, who has counseled hundreds of incest and sexual abuse victims, said, "Every adult who was molested as a child brings from his or her childhood pervasive feelings of being hopelessly inadequate, worthless, and genuinely bad. No matter how different their lives may appear on the surface, all adult victims of incest share a legacy of tragic feelings, The Three D's of incest: Dirty, Damaged, and Different."[4]

In *Healing of Memories,* David Seamands explains why sexual abuse memories are so painful:

> There are many reasons why sexual memories can be painful. The first is that our sexuality is at the very heart of our identity. Our [sexuality] is deeply wrapped up with who we are and how we view ourselves. Damage to this area is bound to deeply affect our self-esteem.
>
> The second reason is that sex is such a powerful emotion...One of the most terrible facts about child molestation is the awakening of such overwhelming emotions at such an early age under such frightening conditions... But perhaps the most important reason these memories are so painful is that sexual feelings can be the most contradictory emotions we humans experience...What [abused women] have undergone can result in their

experiencing sex as an incredible combination of desire and dread, pleasure and pain, fascination and fear. This is why unhealed sexual traumas carried into married life often produce a terrible inner conflict of wanting sex but hating it at the same time."[5]

Let me give you a startling statistic. A study by the U.S. Department of Human Services showed that at least one out of every ten children is molested by a trusted family member before the age of 18.[6] If you are a victim of sexual abuse, please know that you are not alone.

I have always heard people say, "Time heals all wounds." But I disagree. Time does not heal. Only God can heal all wounds.

Mary's Restoration

Could God heal Mary's life, shattered into so many tiny pieces? Can He restore your broken heart? Absolutely!

One day, when Mary was 12 years old, two ladies came to her house and told her about a new church that was opening a few blocks from her house. They invited her to Sunday school and told her that Jesus loved her.

"I was sure they were wrong," Mary said. "No one loved me. I was unlovable."

But the ladies had piqued Mary's interest, and on Sunday morning, while the rest of her household was busy doing other things, Mary snuck away to the storefront church. The people welcomed Mary and even offered to pick her up the following Sunday. However, she did not want to take a chance that the church ladies would encounter her violent mother, so she declined. She would walk.

It was in this tiny Baptist Church of about 50 members that Mary first learned about the amazing love of Jesus Christ. She was introduced to a Savior who knew everything about her and loved her anyway.

"I learned that Jesus would present me to the Father clean and faultless. My heart overflowed when I learned from Jude 24 that He will present me to the Father without fault and with great joy to the only God, my Savior. I marveled at the thought of that dirty little girl of long ago being offered to the Father clean and spotless, like a newborn lamb."

Psalm 27 became Mary's lifeline. "When my father and my mother forsake me, then the LORD will take me up" (Psalm 27:10 KJV). She realized that even though her mother had told her to "get out of the way" her entire life, her heavenly Father was drawing her close. God sent Mary many Christian friends who encouraged her, supported her, and even made sure she could go to college after high school graduation. Through a Christian counselor, Mary was able to face her fears and begin the healing process of years of abuse and neglect. And now? Mary leads support groups for women who have experienced sexual abuse.

"I knew that there were women in my church who most likely had experienced childhood sexual abuse," Mary explained. "This wasn't something that I wanted to tell publicly, but I felt God calling me to make myself available to other hurting women. The most important part of my recovery has been to believe that God really loves me and wants good for my life. When I finally accepted that truth, I was able to reach down inside and put the hurt and pain of the past where it belongs. God's love is a powerful weed killer, and He wanted to kill the weeds of the past that choked the life from my future."

Mary has found peace and purpose in the scars of her past. Now she helps others do the same. While her focus is with women in prisons, she'll share about the God who set her free with anyone who will listen.

God's Healing Salve

When I was a little girl, my grandmother kept a jar of Mentholatum salve at the ready. No matter what the nature of the ailment or the cause, Grandma pulled out the salve and rubbed the slimy goop all over my body. Not only was it slimy, but the smell alone was enough to scare off any germs or bacteria trying to pass the epithelial walls of my skin.

God has a salve as well. It's called forgiveness.

Forgiving those who have hurt or abused us is perhaps one of the most difficult aspects of healing, but without it, I do not believe we can ever be free to find the beauty and purpose in the scars of our pasts. Actually, without extending forgiveness, I believe the wound may not be able to heal at all. Each time we remember what was done to us, what was said and how it was said, and how we were wronged when we were oh so right—we pick at the scab of the offense and reopen the wound.

"Unforgiveness can be likened to a parasite; it feeds on the anger and hurt of its host, finding its most satisfying nourishment in human pain. It thrives on the cycle of replayed scenes, recalled anguish, and rehashed justification for holding fast to grudges. Essentially, unforgiveness grows plump on our desire for revenge."[7]

While many of us don't have a plan to exact revenge, we somehow think that holding on to the unforgiveness is revenge enough. The irony is that the person whom we refuse to forgive most likely doesn't even care or even know we're carrying the unforgiveness around. The only person being hurt when I choose not to forgive is...me. The only person being hurt when you choose not to forgive is...you. It's as if we are hitting our own heads against the wall in order to punish the other person.

The Greek word for forgiveness is *aphieme*. One meaning of the word is to "let go of from one's power, possession, to let go free, to let escape."[8] It means to cut someone loose. So the opposite of forgiveness—unforgiveness—means to tie someone on. Just think about it. When we choose not to forgive, we tie the person to our backs and then lug around the heavy burden of hate, bitterness, or revenge. No wonder some of us are not running the great race of life very well. It's difficult trying to run with all that baggage.

As we move along the journey of discovering peace and purpose in the pain of our past, this is where many decide the terrain grows a bit too rugged to traverse. "That is too hard for me," the weary traveler moans. "I don't like that road," the rebellious sojourner protests. "Isn't there another way?" the reluctant traveler begs.

Unfortunately, forgiveness is the only path to freedom. When you think about it, forgiveness is the only way to freedom for all of us. From the time we were born, each and every one of us are slaves to sin. We didn't become a sinner the first time we did something wrong. We were born in sin with a living body, but a dead spirit. Because of that sin, we were separated from God.

But God didn't leave us as aliens doomed to a life of slavery and eternity in hell. He sent His Son, Jesus Christ, who was born of a virgin, lived a perfect life, died as a sacrifice for our sins, and rose again to reign forever. He didn't wait until we were "good enough," for that day would never come. "While we were still sinners, Christ died for us" (Romans 5:8). God took the biggest obstacle in our lives, our own sinful heritage, and actually changed our spiritual DNA. "If you confess with your mouth, 'Jesus is Lord,' and believe in your heart that God raised him from the dead, you will be saved" (Romans 10:9).

"There is now no condemnation for those who are in Christ Jesus, because through Christ Jesus the law of the Spirit of life set me free from the law of sin and death" (Romans 8:1-2). God sets us free the moment we believe.

But what does that have to do with forgiving the person who hurt us? Everything. The Bible says, "Forgive as the Lord forgave you" (Colossians 3:13).

But he doesn't deserve to be forgiven, I hear you say. Neither did I. Neither did you. Forgiveness has absolutely nothing to do with whether or not the person who hurt us deserves to be forgiven. Forgiveness is not saying that what the person did or didn't do was right. It is simply saying that we are taking the person off our hook and placing them on God's hook. We are cutting them loose from our backs and giving the burden to God. We are no longer allowing them to *hold us captive* by holding a grudge.

As long as we do not forgive, we are held in Satan's trap. It is the number one avenue by which he ensnares his prey. Paul wrote, "Let all bitterness and wrath and anger and clamor and slander be put away from you, along with all malice" (Ephesians 4:31 NASB). Why? "So that no advantage would be taken of us by Satan, for we are not ignorant of his schemes" (2 Corinthians 2:11 NASB).

Forgiveness does not mean that we put ourselves in a position to be abused or mistreated again. If you are in an abusive relationship, it is very important to set up healthy boundaries or remove yourself from the situation. There are many great books to assist with how and when to set boundaries for healthy relationships. One such book is simply titled *Boundaries* by Henry Cloud and John Townsend.

Nothing will make us more bitter than an unforgiving spirit. And nothing will dissolve bitterness more quickly than a decision to forgive and let go of the offense or disappointment. We cannot be bitter and get better at the same time.

Forgiveness is not

- saying that what the person did was not wrong
- absolving the person from responsibility for their actions
- denying that the wrong occurred
- pretending the abuse did not happen

Forgiveness is

- letting go of your need for revenge
- cutting the person loose
- refusing to let bitterness and hatred rule your life
- leaving the past behind by not allowing it to control your actions or emotions

Six Steps to Forgiveness

Forgiveness is hard work. So is mining for gold or unearthing hidden treasure. But in the end, the valuable jewel is worth the effort. Let me walk with you through six steps to forgiveness that might help you in the process.

1. On a piece of paper, write the name of the person who has hurt you.

2. Write down how the person hurt you (rape, verbal abuse, sexual abuse, neglect, betrayal, desertion, rejection).

3. Write down how you feel about that person. Be honest. God knows how you truly feel.

4. Decide to forgive. Forgiveness is not a feeling but a decision of the will. God will never tell us to do something without providing the power to obey. He has told us to forgive, and He will give us the power to do so, but it all begins with the decision to do so.

5. Take your list to God and confess your unforgiveness to Him. "Lord, I come to You today and give up my unforgiveness. I forgive _____ for _____. At this moment, I choose not to hold his or her offense against him or her. I put him or her into Your hands. I pray that You will heal my emotional wounds and help me to be able to help someone else with the same comfort You have given me. I cut _____ loose. Amen."

6. Destroy the list. As a visual exercise, destroy the list. Some have taken the list to a safe place, such as a fireplace, and burned it. Others have actually nailed the paper to a wooden cross. Still others have written the person's name whom they are forgiving on a helium balloon and released it to heaven. However you choose, give the name to God.

Seeing Yourself as God Sees You

Forgiving those who hurt you is one of the highest mountains we must climb on this journey, but it is not the only one. For most of us, the offense has skewed our self-perception, and we fail to see ourselves as God sees us. John wrote, "You will know the truth, and the truth will set you free" (John 8:32). Knowing the truth of who you are in Christ will set you free from a wrong self-perception of who God has created you to be.

For almost 40 years, Margaret lived with word-inflicted wounds that nearly destroyed her life. From the first day she attended her one-room schoolhouse, she and her teacher, Ms. Garner, didn't get along. Ms. Garner was harsh, bitter, and cruel, and she could not tolerate Margaret's childish idiosyncrasies. For years, the tension between the two built up pressure.

Margaret was nine years old when the cataclysmic day occurred—the one that ripped her world apart. It happened after recess when she frantically raced into class, late again. As she burst through the doors, she faced her peers jeering at her maliciously.

"Margaret!" Ms. Garner shouted. "We have been waiting for you! Get up here to the front of the class right now!"

Margaret walked slowly to the teacher's desk, was told to face the class, and then the nightmare began.

Ms. Garner ranted, "Boys and girls, Margaret has been a bad girl. I have tried to help her to be responsible. But, apparently, she doesn't want to learn. So we must teach her a lesson. We must force her to face what a selfish person she has become. I want each of you to come to the front of the room, take a piece of chalk, and write something bad about Margaret on the blackboard. Maybe this experience will motivate her to become a better person!"

Margaret stood frozen next to Ms. Garner. One by one, the students began a silent procession to the blackboard. One by one, they wrote their life-smothering words, slowly extinguishing the light in Margaret's soul. "Margaret is stupid! Margaret is selfish! Margaret is fat! Margaret is a dummy!" On and on they wrote, until 25 terrible scribblings of Margaret's "badness" filled the chalkboard.

The venomous accusations taunted Margaret in what felt like the longest day of her life. After walking home with each caustic word indelibly written on her heart, she crawled into her bed, claimed sickness, and tried to cry the pain away. But the pain never left, and 40 years later she slumped in the waiting room of a psychologist's office, still cringing in the shadow of those 25 sentences.

Jesus understands what it feels like to have people call you names. People called Him a blasphemer (Matthew 9:3), said He was a law breaker (Mark 2:24), and said He had an evil spirit (Mark 3:30). His own family said He was out of His mind (Mark 3:21). Yes, He knows what it feels like to have a broken heart—both figuratively and physically.

After Jesus said, "It is finished" upon the cross of Calvary (John 19:30), the soldiers pierced his side to confirm He was dead. As they removed the spear, water and blood flowed from our Savior's body. Why the water? There is only one explanation. The only way that blood and water could flow from such a wound is if the heart actually burst. Yes, the nails pierced His hands and feet, the crown of thorns dug into His brow, the whip marks tore His flesh, but in the end...Jesus died from a broken heart.

Jesus understands our hurt because He experienced it for Himself. In *The Message,* Eugene Peterson wrote: "Now that we know what we have—Jesus, this great High Priest with ready access to God—let's not let it slip through our fingers. We don't have a priest who is out of touch with our reality. He's been through weakness and testing, experienced it all—all but the sin. So let's walk right up to him and get what he is so ready to give. Take the mercy, accept the help" (Hebrews 4:14-16 MSG).

One More Name

Let's go back to Margaret for a moment. After decades of depression and anxiety, she had finally sought help from a psychologist. Two long years of weekly counseling helped Margaret to finally extricate herself from her past. It had been a long and difficult road, but she smiled at her counselor (how long it had been since she'd smiled!) as they talked about her readiness to move on.

"Well, Margaret," the counselor said softly, "I guess it's graduation day for you. How are you feeling?"

After a long silence, Margaret spoke. "I...I'm okay."

The counselor hesitated. "Margaret, I know this will be difficult, but just to make sure you're ready to move on, I am going to ask you to do something. I want you to go back to your schoolroom and detail the events of that day. Take your time. Describe each of the children as they approach the blackboard. Remember what they wrote and how you felt—all twenty-five students."

In a way, this would be easy for Margaret. For 40 years she had remembered every detail. And yet, to go through the nightmare one more time would take every bit of strength she had. After a long silence, she began the painful description. One by one, she described each of the students vividly, as though she had just seen them, stopping periodically to regain her composure, forcing herself to face each of those students one more time.

Finally, she was finished, and the tears would not stop, could not stop. Margaret cried a long time before she realized someone was whispering her name. "Margaret. Margaret. Margaret." She looked up to see her counselor staring into her eyes, saying her name over and over again. Margaret stopped crying for a moment.

"Margaret. You...you left out one person."

"I certainly did not! I have lived with this story for forty years. I know every student by heart."

"No, Margaret, you did forget someone. See, he's sitting in the back of the classroom. He's standing up, walking toward your teacher, Ms. Garner. She is handing him a piece of chalk and he's taking it, Margaret, he's taking it! Now he's walking over to the blackboard and picking up an eraser. He is erasing every one of the sentences the students wrote. They are gone! Margaret, they are gone! Now he's turning and looking at you, Margaret. Do you recognize him yet? Yes, his name is Jesus. Look, he's writing new sentences on the board. 'Margaret is loved. Margaret is beautiful. Margaret is gentle and kind. Margaret is strong. Margaret has great courage.'"

And Margaret began to weep. But very quickly, the weeping turned into a smile, and then into laughter, and then into tears of joy."[9]

For 40 years Margaret had limped through life with the pain of a broken heart. But finally she allowed Jesus, the Healer, the Comforter, the Great Physician, to bind up her broken heart and allow it to heal.

What is Jesus writing on the chalkboard about you?

You are chosen.

You are dearly loved.

You are holy.

You are beautiful.

You are pure.

You are My bride.

I have your name engraved on the palm of My hand.

Seven

Receiving Grace and Forgiveness

If anyone is in Christ, he is a new creation;
the old has gone, the new has come!
2 Corinthians 5:17

"I just can't believe I did it. I had three abortions and I love children! How could I have killed my children?"

It seemed this question rang in Laura's ears like an alarm clock at the beginning of each day. Even though she had asked God to forgive her several times, Laura had not let go of her past mistakes and forgiven herself.

Not many people know of Laura's abortions. She is a faithful Christian who hides her pain well—except with those who know her best. One day I confronted her.

"Laura, you were a teenager when you had those abortions," I said. "That was thirty years ago and you weren't a Christian. You are a new creation now. The old is gone, the new has come. The Laura you are today would not have an abortion. The old, dead Laura would, but she doesn't exist any longer."

"I know," she replied, "but I can't forgive myself."

For 30 years Laura has operated under a spirit of condemnation. Every time she looks into the eyes of a child, including her own, she feels shame for what she did. However, God forgave Laura years ago. He wiped her slate clean and wrote "forgiven" in bright red letters across the ledger of her life. God longs for Laura to operate under a spirit of grace, mercy, and forgiveness, but He will not force her to open the present, pluck the bow from its lid, and enjoy the gift nestled inside. She must receive it.

Just as clearly as God has forgiven Laura and thrown her sins into the deepest of seas, Satan, the father of lies, reminds her of her failures and encourages her to fish them out day after day. And as long as she is willing to take the bait, he is going to cast the line.

Receiving grace and forgiveness for the wrongs we have committed is an act of faith. "It is difficult to fathom such extravagant, unconditional love, yet so many of us leave His gift unopened. We admire its wrapping or marvel at its enormity, but avoid getting too close. Something within us cannot grasp the idea that God meant this for us, and so we put conditions on accepting His gift."[1] But God puts only one condition on this gift...believe on His Son. God offers the gift of grace, but we must accept it.

No one deserves the grace and mercy of God, but for some reason, He has decided to immerse us in them. In *The Ragamuffin Gospel,* Brennan Manning explains, "To live by grace means to acknowledge my whole life story, the light side and the dark. In admitting my shadow side I learn who I am and what God's grace means. As Thomas Merton put it, 'A saint is not someone who is good but who experiences the goodness of God.'"[2]

In the last chapter, we looked at the wounds in our lives that were inflicted on us by other people, but what about self-inflicted wounds? The poor choices we have made—sexual promiscuity, abortion, lying, cheating, drug abuse, infidelity, murder? These, my friend, can be some of the most difficult wounds to heal. Not difficult for God, mind you, but difficult for us to forgive ourselves. Let me share one of the most incredible stories of grace and forgiveness that God has allowed me to experience. It happened among friends.

Forgiving Karl

Trish Campbell's life was bursting with promise. It was Friday, June 27, 2003. Her son, Wayne, was home from Camden Military Academy in South Carolina. The 16-year-old cadet had just received his driver's license and a new truck. In four days, Trish would be marrying Teddy and then honeymooning on an Alaskan cruise. Life was good.

Wayne had plans to spend the weekend with one of his best friends from the Academy, Karl Kakadelis. Karl had recently graduated from Camden and was scheduled to start classes at The Citadel in the fall.

Trish liked Karl. He seemed to be outgoing, polite, and responsible. She also trusted his parents. His father, Tom, was a pastor at a large church in Charlotte, North Carolina, and his mother, Lindalyn, was a former school board member.

Trish didn't feel comfortable with Wayne driving his new truck out of town in rush hour traffic to Karl's by himself, so she rode along with him as her fiancé followed behind to bring her back home.

"I love you," she said repeatedly before leaving him at the Kakadelis' home.

"I love you too, Mom," he replied as he hugged her several times.

What Trish didn't know was that the boys had a secret.

Nineteen-year-old Karl had planned a party. Because he was

underage, Karl convinced a 21-year-old to purchase a keg of beer for them. The keg was hidden on the grounds of a hotel less than a mile from Karl's home.

Other than a speeding ticket, Karl had never been in trouble. He was an "A" student and graduated second in his class at Camden. He was president of the honor society and the fine arts club, lieutenant governor of the Key Club for North and South Carolina, captain of the soccer and wrestling teams, and company commander to 65 cadets in his senior year. But on June 28, 2003, Karl made some bad decisions.

Karl and his friends had planned the party with precision. He had the place—a nearby field, and alibi—a lie that they were spending the night with a friend.

"You go there and stay there," Tom instructed as the boys prepared to leave the house.

"And no alcohol," Lindalyn added with her finger pointed at their faces.

"Oh, no, ma'am," they replied. "We don't drink."

After they left, Lindalyn said, "Tom, I'm worried. Something doesn't feel right. Those boys were too cocky."

The boys went to the hotel sometime after 10:00 PM and picked up the keg. Karl drove a jeep while Wayne held the beer in his lap. When they reached the designated party spot, friends began to congregate. Several kids brought tents and built a bonfire.

Karl controlled who drank and how much they drank. They had all agreed that they would not drive after drinking.

Around midnight, Karl got a call on his cell phone.

"Hey, man, this is Chris," the caller said. "I've got the ice, but I can't find the field." Then he explained where he was.

"You're only a mile or so away," Karl said. "Stay there and I'll come and lead you over here."

"Karl, I don't think you should drive," one of his friends called out.

"I'm okay," he yelled back.

Karl jumped into the jeep and buckled in. Another boy climbed in the passenger seat and also buckled his seat belt. The convertible top was down, and Wayne jumped in the back, holding on to the roll bar.

Karl made a loop around the bonfire and then headed across the field and onto the road. About a quarter of a mile from the party, Karl's Jeep drifted left. He overcorrected and cut a hard right and then back to the left. The Jeep and the driver were out of control. The right-side tires blew and the rims dug into the road. Then the Jeep flipped and ejected Wayne about 50 feet onto the pavement.

The Jeep landed off the road on its right side in a patch of briars and weeds. Wayne was lying in the road, his face in a pool of blood. Karl and the other boy were still in the car but badly injured. Karl's upper lip was torn and hanging, but he still did not understand the gravity of the situation. For the first time he realized that he might be drunk.

Karl stumbled over to his best friend, Wayne, and tried to talk to him, but he only heard moans.

The tranquility of early Sunday morning, June 28, 2003, was pierced by sirens, the swooshing of a rescue helicopter, and the wailing of young adults. As the helicopter airlifted Wayne to the hospital, Karl and the other passenger rode in the ambulance. Meanwhile, calls to parents were made.

Both sets of parents were a mixture of anger, hurt, disbelief, and concern. When Tom caught a glimpse of Trish at the hospital, they embraced and cried. It was ten hours before Trish was allowed to see her son. Meanwhile, she held on to images of her handsome boy with dark hair, brownish-green eyes, and military posture. In her head she could hear echoes of him singing hymns with her in the car.

Finally, Trish was allowed to see Wayne. His head was bandaged and bruised, and tubes wove in and out of his body.

Karl had surgery to reattach his lip, but there was no immediate help for the internal injuries on his soul. His heart was broken. He was broken.

"I am so sorry," Karl cried when he saw his best friend's mom. "I am so sorry."

"I don't blame you," Trish said. "We all make bad decisions. When Wayne gets out of here, he is going to have some explaining to do."

But Wayne never left the hospital. Six days after he had arrived, Wayne Campbell, the only son of Trish Campbell, died.

At the funeral home visitation, Karl buried his face in his father's chest and wept uncontrollably. Trish, seeing Karl in the other room, walked over and sat down beside him.

"I am so sorry. I am so sorry!" he cried.

Trish cupped Karl's tearstained face in her hands. "Honey, I forgive you. I love you. Wayne loved you."

Those who heard and saw the interaction were startled at such forgiveness and grace pouring from one woman. It was not human...it was divine.

Later Trish explained. "I am a sinner, and God sent His only Son to save me and forgive me of my sins. I'm not worthy of that forgiveness. So why wouldn't I forgive Karl?"

Where Do We Go from Here?

Karl turned himself in to the authorities. He was fingerprinted, booked, and faced a 59-month jail term for involuntary manslaughter. The police were amazed at his parents. "They didn't try to get him out of the mess he was in. They wanted everything out in the open so others could learn from his mistakes. Regardless of what the court decided Karl's punishment would be, he would live with a life sentence knowing that he had played a part in his best friend's death.

Karl's day in court was postponed for seven months. While he waited, he lived with confusion and pain. His dreams of going to The Citadel and becoming an Air Force pilot were destroyed. While speaking to a group of high school students, Karl said, "I tell you one way I serve my time right now. I live with Wayne in my heart and with that accident on my mind all the time. I guess my punishment is to know that I made a mistake that cost my best friend his life."

On March 11, 2004, Karl had his day in court. Before the proceedings began, Wayne's mother, Trish, walked over to Karl, leaned forward, and kissed him. "Karl, I have to sit on the other side today, but I am praying for you. You keep praying too," she whispered.

One by one, men and women stood and testified on Karl's behalf—his soccer coach, his teachers, and his Sunday school teacher. After the prosecutor presented his case, Trish asked if she could address the court. Permission was granted.

"My son and Karl went to school together and were best friends," Trish began. "I love this boy like my own child. It's not my wish that he should serve prison time. I understand that he will have some type of punishment, and I accept that. But I know Karl is truly remorseful and never intended for this to happen."

When the courtroom was silent, the judge looked at the broken boy and said, "Where are your accusers? No one wants you to go to jail. I cannot send you to jail."

Karl's sentence was determined: a 13- to 16-month suspended sentence, three years probation, 50 hours of community service, 20 hours of counseling, public addresses to Camden Military Academy for the next three years, and six speeches to area high schools for the next three years. No jail time.

Yes, Karl avoided a prison cell, but he still didn't feel free.

Several weeks later, Camden Military Academy held an outdoor memorial service for Wayne. It was three days before Wayne would have graduated. Karl stood at the back of the crowd, leaning against a pine tree, his head lowered and arms crossed. When the ceremony ended, Kenny, Wayne's father, hugged Karl and then pushed a finger in Karl's chest.

"Keep telling your story," Kenny said. "Don't do it just because the court told you to do it. Continue to do it after that. You've got an education now. Use it."

Since then, Karl has seen a plastic surgeon to fix his lip. But he chose to keep the scar on his hand. He wants to keep it as a reminder of what a bad decision can do to destroy a life.[3]

It was difficult for me to write this story. It took me several days. Why? Because as I typed, my eyes filled with tears and blurred my vision. I'd stop. Go back the next day. Try again. Tears.

I know this family. I know this story. My heart breaks even still thinking of precious Karl and the pain he has had to suffer for one bad choice. But you know what? We all make bad choices every day. His simply came at a high price.

I see myself in Karl. While I haven't been convicted of involuntary manslaughter while impaired, I've done other things that have been detrimental to people's souls...and to my own. And then I see Wayne's mother approach the bench on Karl's behalf. I see Jesus approach the bench on my behalf.

"Judge," He would say. "I love this woman as though she were My own...she *is* My own. I know that she will have to face consequences here on earth for the poor choices she has made, but I do not want her to serve any jail time. I ask that you extend mercy and grace to this woman, that you commute her sentence and set her free."

Then the gavel comes down and the judge announces: "No jail time."

Yes, the Judge has set me free. I gratefully accept His grace and forgiveness. But I also see another scene...Wayne's daddy...my heavenly Father...pointing His finger at my chest and saying "Keep telling your story. Don't do it just because the court told you to do it. Continue to do it after that. You've got an education now. Use it."

That's what this book is all about. We've got an education... now we need to use it.

Brokenness and Repentance

All through the Bible we see amazing examples of God's grace and forgiveness extended to weak human beings like you and me. King David was one such man.

God referred to David as a "man after my own heart" (Acts 13:22). I can't think of a better endorsement than that. And yet David got caught up in his own press and, for a moment, thought he was above the laws of God.

One spring, at the time when the kings went out to war, King David decided to stay behind and relax at the palace. While walking on the roof to get a breath of fresh air, he caught sight of his beautiful neighbor, Bathsheba, taking a bath on her roof. He looked. He saw. He wanted.

"Who is that girl?" he asked one of his servants.

"That, my lord, is the wife of Uriah the Hittite, one of your faithful soldiers."

"Send someone and bring her to me!" he commanded.

So one starry night, in the heat of passion, David slept with his neighbor's wife and she conceived a child.

When David received word that Bathsheba was pregnant, he panicked. Did David confess? No. Did David repent? No. Instead, he tried to cover his tracks. He sent for Uriah to come home from battle, thinking that he would sleep with his wife and thus conceal the fact that the child she bore was David's. But the faithful Uriah would not indulge himself in such pleasure during a time of war. Rather than enjoy the comfort of his wife's embrace, Uriah slept outside the palace door.

So David went to Plan B.

He sent a message to Joab, the commander of the army.

"When you go to war, place Uriah on the front lines. Then, when the battle ensues, have the men retreat, leaving Uriah exposed as a lone target for the enemy."

Joab followed the commander in chief's request. Uriah was left alone on the front lines and killed. After the proper time of mourning, David took the pregnant widow as his wife (2 Samuel 11:1-26).

Do you wonder how David, a man after God's own heart, was

feeling about this time? Was he afraid? Was he remorseful? Was he proud of himself for the great cover-up?

Fortunately, God has allowed us to see inside this man's heart. After this time of moral failure, David penned Psalm 51.

> Have mercy on me, O God,
> according to your unfailing love;
> according to your great compassion
> blot out my transgressions.
> Wash away all my iniquity
> and cleanse me from my sin.
> For I know my transgressions,
> and my sin is always before me.
> Against you, you only, have I sinned
> and done what is evil in your sight,
> so that you are proved right when you speak
> and justified when you judge.
> Surely I was sinful at birth,
> sinful from the time my mother conceived me.
> Surely you desire truth in the inner parts;
> you teach me wisdom in the inmost place.
> Cleanse me with hyssop, and I will be clean;
> wash me, and I will be whiter than snow.
> Let me hear joy and gladness;
> let the bones you have crushed rejoice.
> Hide your face from my sins
> and blot out all my iniquity.
> Create in me a pure heart, O God,
> and renew a steadfast spirit within me.
> Do not cast me from your presence
> or take your Holy Spirit from me.
> Restore to me the joy of your salvation
> and grant me a willing spirit, to sustain me.
> Then I will teach transgressors your ways,

> and sinners will turn back to you.
> Save me from bloodguilt, O God,
> the God who saves me,
> and my tongue will sing of your righteousness.
> O Lord, open my lips,
> and my mouth will declare your praise.
> You do not delight in sacrifice, or I would bring it;
> you do not take pleasure in burnt offerings.
> The sacrifices of God are a broken spirit;
> a broken and contrite heart,
> O God, you will not despise.
> PSALM 51:1-17

David was crushed in spirit—and yet no one knew. Or did they?

After David had taken Bathsheba to be his wife, the prophet Nathan confronted David with his sin.

David did not try to justify his actions, place blame on anyone else, or claim amnesty because he was king. Immediately he said, "I have sinned against the LORD."

After David repented, Nathan proclaimed, "The LORD has taken away your sin" (2 Samuel 12:13).

David was a broken man who repented of his sin and then immediately received grace and forgiveness from God. He resumed his duties as king and proceeded to become one of the most powerful kings in Israel's history.

Forgiving the Reflection in the Mirror

David was able to accept God's forgiveness, but for many, guilt lingers like an arthritic pain that throbs with the changing of the weather. On the sunny days of our lives, we congratulate ourselves for moving past the shadows in the closet. Then, on the cloudy days, when the storms of life threaten, the winds of adversity blow, and the lightning bolts of remembrance strike, we cower in shame. I believe that this roller coaster of emotions occurs when we place the responsibility of clearing the slate of mistakes on ourselves rather than on the only One who can truly wipe them away. We saddle ourselves with conditions that were never imposed by God.

Here's the truth of it. There is nothing we can do to *earn* God's forgiveness. Nothing. It's not about us. It's all about Him. It's only when we "accept ownership of our powerlessness and helplessness, when we acknowledge that we are paupers at the door of God's mercy, [that] God can make something beautiful out of us."[4]

There is a healthy guilt and an unhealthy guilt. In *The Raga-muffin Gospel,* Brennan Manning explains the difference:

> Preoccupation with self is always a major component of unhealthy guilt and recrimination. It stirs our emotions, churning in self-destructive ways, closes us in upon the mighty citadel of self, leads to depression and despair and preempts the presence of a compassionate God. The language of unhealthy guilt is harsh. It is demanding, abusing, criticizing, rejecting, accusing, blaming, condemning, reproaching and scolding. It is one of impatience and chastisement. Christians are shocked and horrified because they have failed. Unhealthy guilt becomes bigger than life. The image of the childhood story "Chicken Little" comes to mind. Guilt becomes the experience in which people feel the sky is falling.
>
> Yes, we feel guilt over sins, but healthy guilt is one which acknowledges the wrong done and feels remorse, but then is free to embrace the forgiveness that has been offered. Healthy guilt focuses on the realization that all has been forgiven, the wrong has been redeemed.[5]

Paul said it this way: "Godly sorrow brings repentance that leads to salvation and leaves no regret, but worldly sorrow brings death" (2 Corinthians 7:10). Satan uses guilt to condemn us. God uses conviction to bring us to repentance and forgiveness.

Pride and Self-Righteousness

Now let's go back a few years in history to David's predecessor, King Saul. This was a time in Israel's history when God ruled the people and spoke through the prophets. This type of governing is known as a theocracy. But after a while, the people grew tired of being ruled by God. They decided they wanted a king to rule over them...just like all the other nations. So God allowed them to have a king and appointed a man named Saul from the tribe of Benjamin. At first, Saul was terrified of his new assignment. As a matter of fact, at his coronation, they found him hiding among the baggage! (1 Samuel 10:20-23). But eventually he settled into his new role and began enjoying all the perks.

God anointed Saul with the Holy Spirit, and he even received the gift of prophesy. He led Israel into victory on several battlefields and depended on God for wisdom and strength...for a while.

But after a few months, Saul's confidence rose to the danger level, and he began to take matters into his own hands. Before going to battle against the Philistines, Saul and his men were waiting on the prophet Samuel to offer needed sacrifices to the Lord. After seven days, the time set by Samuel the prophet himself, Saul grew tired of waiting and his men began to get restless.

How hard can it be? thought Saul. *I'll just offer the sacrifice myself.*

So he went against the commands of God and made himself a priest.

Samuel arrived just as Saul was putting the finishing touches on the altar.

"What have you done?" Samuel exclaimed.

"It's all your fault," Saul protested. "When you didn't come, the men started shaking in their sandals and scattering like flies. I had to do something! So I offered the sacrifice myself."

Saul didn't admit that he had done anything wrong. Rather, he justified his actions, placed the blame on someone else, and held his head high (1 Samuel 13:5-12).

And that was the beginning of the end for Saul.

Did he learn his lesson? Oh, no. Just a few chapters later, we see that he disobeyed God once again. God told him to go into battle against the Amalekites and destroy every living thing, taking no plunder for himself. However, during the attack, he spared the Amalekite king and kept the best sheep, cattle, and everything that was good.

Once again the prophet Samuel confronted Saul.

"I did everything the Lord commanded," Saul boasted. (As though God wouldn't know the difference.)

"Oh, yeah?" Samuel replied. "Then what's that baa-baa noise I hear in the background?"

"Oh, that. Well, we did take the best of the sheep and the cattle...to offer sacrifices to the Lord, you understand."

Once again, Saul did not show any remorse for what he had done. Once again he justified his actions, placed blame on someone else, and held his head high.

"Stop it! Just stop it!" Samuel yelled in frustration. "God doesn't want your sacrifices. He wants you to obey Him. Haven't you figured that out by now?"

Unlike David, Saul was not sorry for what he had done. He was just sorry he got caught.

As a result, God took Saul's kingdom away. He was finished (see 1 Samuel 15:1-23).

Receiving God's grace and forgiveness has everything to do with our heart attitude toward the sin. "God opposes the proud but gives grace to the humble" (James 4:6).

Grace and Forgiveness

It seems that David's sin was much more blatant than Saul's. And yet God took the throne away from Saul and gave David a full pardon. What was the difference? David was repentant, remorseful, and broken. Saul was arrogant, argumentative, and prideful.

Where are you on the continuum of pride and brokenness? God

wants us to be broken over our sins, but then He takes those broken pieces and binds us back together to make us stronger and more useful than ever before. As long as we are clinging to the pieces of our broken lives, they remain just that...broken pieces.

Won't you open your clenched fist and offer your shattered past as a sacrifice to the Savior? He will heal you. He will use you. He will make you stronger than before.

I've learned that a broken bone that has mended is strongest at its place of healing. Likewise, scar tissue is tougher and more resilient than virgin flesh. God can take the wounds of our lives and make us stronger than before.

C.S. Lewis observed:

> For God is not merely mending, not simply restoring a status quo. Redeemed humanity is to be something more glorious than unfallen humanity would have been...The greater the sin, the greater the mercy: the deeper the death, the brighter the rebirth.[6]

Saul's light was snuffed out. David's shone brighter than before.

Before Jesus went to the cross, He served His disciples their last meal together. He broke bread, which represented His body, and passed a cup of wine, which represented His blood. This sacrament, often referred to as the Lord's Supper, has been celebrated for centuries. Isn't it interesting that both the wine and the bread are made through crushing—both grain and grapes. Could it be that our lives, through crushing and brokenness, serve as a living testimony of what Christ has done in us?

"The closest communion with God comes, I believe, through the sacrament of tears. Just as grapes are crushed to make wine and grain to make bread, so the elements of this sacrament come from the crushing experience of life."[7]

Paid in Full

When we ask God to forgive us of our past mistakes and failures,

He does. The Bible promises, "If we confess our sins, he is faithful and just and will forgive us our sins and purify us from all unrighteousness" (1 John 1:9). We confess our sins, receive forgiveness, and believe that it is finished. In the last chapter, we looked at the Greek word for forgiveness, *aphieme*. While it does mean to "cut one loose," it also means "to cancel a debt, the remission of the punishment due to sinful conduct."[8]

It involves confession and repentance. To "confess" means more than saying, "Yes, I did it." In the New Testament, the word "confess" is *homologeo* and means "to speak the same thing, to assent, accord, agree with...to confess by way of admitting oneself guilty of what one is accused of, the result of inward conviction."[9] Like David's confession, it is agreeing with God about your sin.

To "repent" means to change your mind and go in the opposite direction. The Greek word is *metanoeo* and signifies "to change one's mind or purpose."[10] When Jesus forgave the woman caught in adultery, He said, "Go and sin no more" (John 8:11 NKJV). In other words, "Stop what you're doing, go in the opposite direction, and don't commit adultery again." That is a picture of true repentance.

Are you brokenhearted over your sin? Have you asked God to forgive you? Have you agreed with God that what you did was wrong, and are you committed to turn and go in the opposite direction? If you have asked, then He has forgotten the offense already. If you have asked, but are having difficulty receiving freedom, then pray this prayer and receive freedom by faith:

> *Dear Lord, I come before You today, confessing _____ _____. I am truly repentant and sorry for my sin against You. I ask that You forgive me and cleanse me. Right now, I receive Your grace and forgiveness. I believe that You have forgiven me and no longer hold my sin against me. I accept the sacrifice Jesus made on the cross for my sin and I thank You that my debt has been paid in full. Thank You, God, for forgiving me. In Jesus' name. Amen.*

Now, dear one, I want you to picture your sin nailed to the cross. It is finished. Don't let Satan try to convince you otherwise. And believe me, he will. Satan is called "the accuser" because he accuses Christians day and night (Revelation 12:10). I picture him walking back and forth with our mug shots before the throne of God, saying, "Look at her! She's guilty as sin!" And in response our heavenly Father says, "I know her. She's my precious child whom I love. Her sentence has already been taken care of. She's forever free."

Second Chances

Perhaps one of the most memorable and heart-touching stories of grace and forgiveness is recorded in Luke 15. It's what we've come to know as the Story of the Prodigal Son. This young man demanded his inheritance while his father was still alive, spent it all on riotous living, and found himself dirty, destitute, and despairing. As despicable as pigs were to Jews, this young man took a job taking care of pigs and eating their food just to stay alive. But then he had an epiphany.

"When he came to his senses, he said, 'How many of my father's hired men have food to spare, and here I am starving to death. I will set out and go back to my father and say to him: Father, I have sinned against heaven and against you. I am no longer worthy to be called your son; make me like one of your hired men.' So he got up and went to his father" (Luke 15:17-20).

And where was his father? He was panning the horizon, hoping for a sign that his boy might return home. While "he was still a long way off" (verse 20), the father spotted his son on the horizon. Filled with compassion, he picked up the edges of his robe and ran. He didn't wait for his son to come to him, grovel at his feet, and beg for forgiveness. No, as soon as the father caught a glimpse of his son, he dashed toward his boy, smothered him with kisses, and welcomed him home.

If you remember, not everyone was happy when the prodigal

son returned. His big brother resented the fact that he got another chance. And you know what? There will be those who resent the fact that we get another chance as well.

"Big brother won't mind if you come back as long as you hang your head and wear your shame. But when God has the audacity to give you a little dignity back and you dare lift your radiant face to heaven in liberated praise, big brother may be appalled!...It's pride that can't celebrate with a prodigal-come-home. Folks who won't celebrate are still kidding themselves into thinking they did something right to be loved by their Father."[11]

I say, let him be appalled. Nothing makes some people angrier than grace. Big brother is invited to the party too, and it's his decision whether or not he wants to join in the celebration. I'm just glad he's not the one in charge.

Seeing Yourself as God Sees You

I'd like to end this chapter the same way that I ended chapter 6—seeing yourself as God sees you. This is so important to me because for many years after I became a Christian, I operated under a false sense of who I really was. I had no idea of the change that occurred in me the moment I accepted Christ. I did not see myself as God saw me, and I had no idea His truth was different from my perception of it. Over my mind was a grid system, like a sieve, of inferiority, insecurity, and inadequacy. When I processed information about my world and about myself, it had to first filter through that negative grid system.

It was not until my thirties that I began to realize that how God saw me and how I saw me were very different. Like a hungry child, I began to research and write down verses about my new identity in Christ. I learned that I was fearfully and wonderfully made (Psalm 139:14), a child of God (John 1:12), totally free (John 8:36), chosen (John 15:16), a son [daughter] of God (Romans 8:14), a new creation (2 Corinthians 5:17), a saint (Ephesians 1:1), righteous and holy (Ephesians 4:24), dearly loved (Colossians 3:12), and completely forgiven (1 John 1:9). I also learned that it was Satan who held that negative grid system in place.

I came to a crossroads in my spiritual journey. I could continue believing the lies or I could begin believing the truth. Jesus said, "You will know the truth, and the truth will set you free" (John 8:32). I decided to believe the truth. It was difficult and didn't feel comfortable at first. Like the lame man who regained the movement of his legs, or the blind man who received his sight, I had to adjust to my new belief system.

Oh, my friend, God has so much planned for us to do and to be, but if we are operating with a false sense of who we really are, we may be paralyzed by feelings of guilt and shame.

On Jesus' first day of public ministry, He walked down to the river and was baptized by His cousin John. As Jesus came out of the water, a voice came from heaven: "You are my Son, whom I love; with you I am well pleased" (Luke 3:22). That is the same thing God says to you...and to me.

"You are my child...whom I love...with you I am well pleased."

"You cannot get beyond your own opinion of yourself—no matter how many good things God may say about you in His Word. Regardless of all the wonderful plans God may have for your life, none of them will come to pass without your cooperation."[12] God extends grace and forgiveness. It is up to us to accept it and believe.

EIGHT

Renouncing the Cloud of Shame

Those who look to him are radiant;
their faces are never covered with shame.
PSALM 34:5

The table was deathly cold, as were the doctor's hands that were swiftly at work to remove the small life whose heart had only just begun to beat. The room was spinning, and the shame of what I was allowing him to do to my baby threatened to choke the life out of me as well. Although there was no sound, no verbal plea, I could still hear an ever-so-small voice calling out to me in my despair. What was it saying? No, please don't. Please don't. Please don't.

But it was too late. The voice was gone, along with the tiny little body. The same guilt, the depression, and the total sense of despair followed me as I left the room. How could I do such a selfish and

117

wicked thing? I thought. What kind of human being am I? I just wanted to die.

As I staggered to the exit door of the clinic, I noticed a nurse filing a card in her drawer. I supposed it had my name and the information concerning my dead baby. So that's it, I thought. His entire life is on an index card that will remain shoved between the E's and the G's in that cold metal filing cabinet. What did the card say? Did it say if the baby was a boy or a girl? Call it intuition, but I believe it was a boy.

In the days and weeks that followed, I pictured God's hands forming my baby's features, his personality, his likes and his dislikes. Then I would tell myself to stop thinking about it...it didn't matter. But somehow, I knew it did matter. I knew that something that mattered so very much was written on a card instead of living, breathing, laughing, and loving. The card will never tell about the expression on his face when he takes his first steps or pedals a bike for the first time. The card will never tell about the many nights I would have crept into his room after he had gone to sleep just to hold his sleeping body in my arms or the way I smiled over his messy hair when he woke up in the morning.

That little boy will never know butterfly kisses or experience the sheer delight of his daddy arriving home from work. He'll never know the warmth and security of cuddling with his mama after a bath. No, the card will not tell of these things because they will never happen.

—Ginger

Ginger is a brown-eyed beauty—a petite 5'3", 100 pounds of love for Jesus. But that wasn't always her story.

From the time Ginger was born, her parents adored her. They were both lavish and lenient. On her sixteenth birthday Ginger received a car with a tag on the front that said it well: "Spoiled Rotten."

During Ginger's teenage years, her parents became interested in the Christian faith and both made a commitment to Jesus Christ. For the first time, church became an important part of their family life. Ginger was not happy about this change. The freedom she had always enjoyed was now filtered through her parents' new-found faith. *If I'm going to have to go to church,* Ginger thought, *then I'm going to find the best-looking, wildest guy there to date.* And that's exactly what she did.

"I still remember the ache in my stomach the night my best friend and I sat on my bed waiting to see if the stick turned pink," Ginger said. "It did."

Ginger was a senior in high school...and pregnant.

One week later, Ginger, along with her boyfriend, walked out of an abortion clinic, both realizing they had just made the most terrible mistake of their lives. In just a few moments, and for $200, their child was dead.

For many years, Ginger stuffed the shame and searing pain of what she had done into a secret place with the invisible key dangling from her neck. Her family didn't understand her periods of depression, the times of quiet reflection, and bouts of unexplained tears. When Ginger saw babies or small children cry...she would cry. *Is that what the baby felt like when he was torn from my body?* she wondered.

Nightmares of dead babies haunted Ginger night after sleepless night. She knew she had to tell someone—but whom?

Finally, Ginger confided in a man who worked at her parents' restaurant. She knew he was a Christian and could be trusted.

"Ginger," Sam said, "what you did was wrong, but God will forgive you if you ask."

"I don't deserve to be forgiven," she cried.

"Nope, none of us do," he reassured her. "That's what grace means, receiving forgiveness that we don't deserve. And you also need to forgive yourself."

"I don't think I could ever do that," she mumbled through her sobs.

"I think the first thing you need to do is tell your parents," Sam said. "You'll never be free until you do."

Then Sam held Ginger's hands and prayed for her. Even though the wound was still open and bleeding, the smallest glimmer of healing had begun.

A few nights later, Ginger crept into her parents' bedroom.

"Mom, Dad, I have something I need to tell you," Ginger whimpered.

"Come on in, honey," her mom said as she reached over to turn on a bedside lamp.

"No! Don't turn on the light!" Ginger begged.

The next few moments seemed like an eternity. Ginger crawled up in her parents' bed, nuzzled in between them, and told the entire story of the pregnancy, the abortion, and the lingering guilt and pain. For hours they cried and held their little girl.

Ginger also asked God to forgive her, and eventually she forgave herself. Jesus wiped away her shame and replaced her tattered rags with a robe of righteousness which she wears today. No longer does she have the key to her shame dangling from her neck. It now belongs to the Master of her heart.

Today, Ginger is one of God's mighty warriors. She is a speaker and a writer who is having a great impact all around the world. She warns people about one of the greatest lies of the twentieth century—that abortion is a solution to an unwanted pregnancy. Ginger speaks on behalf of the unborn, and tells of the redemptive power of a loving God who can forgive the sin of murder and even use a terrible decision to bring glory to Himself.

Statistics show that one in four women in the church today have had an abortion. They desperately need someone who is not ashamed of her scars to tell them about the forgiveness and love of God. But they don't want to hear it from someone who has not felt the condemnation themselves. "Forgiveness? That's easy for you," they silently scoff. "You haven't done what I've done."

But because Ginger is not ashamed of her scars, she boldly tells her story, and women see hope displayed before them. God is using Ginger to bind up the brokenhearted and set the captive free.

The Origin of Shame

"In the beginning God created the heavens and the earth" (Genesis 1:1). No matter how many times I hear those words, my heart quickens with awe. To think that before God spoke the world into being, there was...nothing. But then God said, "Let there be light" (verse 3), and it was so. Over the next six days God painted the sky, gathered the water together to form the seas, and blew a fresh wind to make dry ground. He spoke and vegetation of every kind sprang forth from the ground, the sun appeared in the sky by day, and the man in the moon said his first hello. God stocked the seas with living creatures, the skies with winged foul, and the earth with all things that creep and crawl.

On the sixth day, God decided to make a creature unlike any He had created before—one in His own image. So rather than speak it into existence as He had done with all of His other creations, God bent down and gathered a bit of dust from the earth. And from that dust, the fingertips of God shaped and molded man.

At the end of each day, God looked at what He had made and said, "It is good." The only time He said, "It is *not* good," was when He said, "It is not good for the man to be alone" (Genesis 2:18).

So God caused the man to fall into a deep sleep, took one of his ribs, and fashioned a helpmate for him. His final masterpiece, a grand finale of sorts, was woman. And on the seventh day, God rested.

God called the man Adam. Then, in keeping with Adam's chore of naming all the animals, Adam named the woman Eve. They were perfect and had the perfect life. They had a sense of great significance as rulers over all the creatures of the entire earth, they were safe and secure in their relationship with God as their provider, and they had a sense of belonging in complete union with God and each other. The Bible tells us that in the Garden of Eden, they were *naked and unashamed* (Genesis 2:25).

Adam and Eve had free reign over the entire Garden, with only one restriction: "You are free to eat from any tree in the garden; but you must not eat from the tree of the knowledge of good and evil, for when you eat of it you will surely die" (Genesis 2:16-17).

But pretty soon Satan came slithering into Adam and Eve's utopic world. Cunningly, he tempted Eve with the one restriction placed on her by God. He made her think that God was holding out on her...which is his favorite MO.

> First, he questioned God: "Did God really say, 'You must not eat from any tree in the garden?'" (Genesis 3:1).
> Second, he denied God: "You will not surely die!" (verse 4).
> Third, he caused her to doubt God's justice: "For God knows that when you eat of it your eyes will be opened, and you will be like God, knowing good and evil" (Genesis 3:5).

Eve believed the lies of the deceiver and ate the forbidden fruit. Then she gave it to her husband, and he ate it too. "Then the eyes of both of them were opened, and they realized they were naked; so they sewed fig leaves together and made coverings for themselves" (Genesis 3:7). At the very moment Eve sank her teeth into the forbidden fruit, fear and shame entered the world, their relationship with God was broken, and their spirits died.

Adam and Eve immediately tried to cover their shame by sewing fig leaves together to make aprons. When that wasn't enough, they tried to hide from God among the trees of the garden. The next day, God came to take his early morning stroll with his beloved children, but they were nowhere to be found. So He called out to them: "Where are you?"

That was the first question in the Bible, and it is still God's question to us today: "Where are you?" No matter what we've done to cause us to want to hide our faces from God, He calls us out of hiding and into His arms. "Where are you, My child? Come to Me."

He [Adam] answered, "I heard you in the garden, and I was afraid because I was naked; so I hid." And he said, "Who told you that you were naked? Have you eaten from the tree that I commanded you not to eat from?" The man said, "The woman you put here with me—she gave me some fruit from the tree, and I ate it." Then the LORD God said to the woman, "What is this you have done?" The woman said, "The serpent deceived me, and I ate" (Genesis 3:10-13).

Because of their disobedience, God cursed the serpent, condemned Adam and Eve to a life of trouble and toil, and cast them out of the Garden of Eden forever. But God had a plan to reunite fallen mankind to Himself. In *A Gift for All People,* Max Lucado wrote, "The moment the forbidden fruit touched the lips of Eve, the shadow of the cross appeared on the horizon. And between that moment and the moment the man with the mallet placed the spike against the wrist of God, a master plan was fulfilled."

Adam and Eve brought sin and shame into the world in the Garden of Eden, but Jesus Christ made a way for it to be removed in the Garden of Gethsemane. Adam and Eve disobeyed God by eating of the forbidden tree, and Jesus Christ gave His life as a sacrifice to eradicate that shame by hanging on Calvary's tree. He paid the price so that we could live with God throughout eternity.

Signals of Shame

Before we start singing and dancing for joy because of what Jesus has done for us, let's go back to the Garden of Eden for just a moment and notice the characteristics of shame. From the first time shame entered the world until today, it looks the same, feels the same, and has the same effect on all mankind.

1. *Shame hides.* Adam and Eve hid from God. Shame causes us to hide our true selves from the world.

2. *Shame denies.* Adam and Eve both denied they had done anything wrong.

3. *Shame blames.* Rather than admit their failure, Adam blamed Eve, Eve blamed Satan, and Satan just smiled.

4. *Shame tries to cover up.* Adam and Eve tried to cover up their sin with fig leaves. We put on a happy face and try to cover up our shame with clothes, activities, achievements, and any number of window dressings.

5. *Shame causes fear.* After they sinned, Adam and Eve hid from God because they feared what He would do to them. When we feel shame, we fear what would happen if someone were to discover the truth.

If you notice any of these characteristics of shame in your life, please know that God wants to remove them. When Jesus died on the cross, His blood ran over the cursed thorns and onto the ground below. What a beautiful picture of Jesus' blood covering the very curse...the thorns...that were part of man's punishment from the Garden of Eden.

Remember Pig Pen from the Peanuts cartoon strip? Some of us have been walking around like Pig Pen in a cloud of shame that surrounds us wherever we go. God wants us to step out from that cloud. It is Satan who tries to hold the mantle of shame around us like Pig Pen's dust cloud. "If he can't make us unclean, he will at least do everything he can do to make us feel unclean."[1] But if we continue to live in shame and believe Satan's condemnation over God's forgiveness—we are choosing to believe a lie.

The Hidden Key

When I was a teenager, my high school was just a few miles from my home. Lunch break was a bit less than an hour, but I enjoyed driving home and taking a respite from the hustle and bustle of the crowded hallways.

Rocky Mount, North Carolina, was a sleepy little town with

a railroad track that ran down the middle of downtown dividing it into two counties, a fledgling minor league baseball team that ranked in *Sports Illustrated* as having the worst housing conditions in the league, and a Hardee's fast-food restaurant on every corner reminding us that the corporate office for the chain was just down the street. When I was a child, we slept with our windows open, doors unlocked, and rode our bicycles all over town without a hint of reservation.

But times changed in the late '60s and early '70s. We began to keep our windows closed at night, doors locked even during the day, and kids stayed much closer to home. At our house, we kept an extra key in the mailbox just inside the garage. The garage had no door, so the mailbox was accessible to anyone. But the only people who knew the key was in the mailbox was our family and the mailman.

In high school, when I went home for lunch at 12:10 every day, I simply reached in the mailbox to retrieve the key, and then placed it back in the box until I came home again at 3:15.

One day I came home after school at the usual time, used the hidden key, and let myself in. Before grabbing a snack, I made a beeline to the television to turn on my favorite program. When I opened the door, I realized the TV was missing.

I didn't know anything was wrong with the TV, I thought. *Mom must have taken it into the shop for repairs.*

I called Mom at her craft store.

"Hello, Bee N' Beetle, can I help you?"

"Hey, Mom. This is Sharon. Did you take the TV in for repair?"

"No, I didn't. Why?"

"Well, because it isn't here."

"What do you mean it isn't there?"

"It's not here. The cabinet is empty."

"Is anything else missing?" she asked with a hint of fear in her voice.

"I don't know. Let me check."

I didn't have to look far to see that a few other items were gone. When I came back to the phone to report, Mom said, "Sharon, quick! Get out of there!"

When the police came, we discovered that someone had indeed entered our house and taken many things. And how did he get in? Why, he used the hidden key.

Apparently, someone had been watching me. He knew that I came home at 12:10 and left again at 12:45. He also knew that I came home from school around 3:15. So between 12:45 and 3:15, he simply took the key from the mailbox, let himself in, and helped himself to whatever he so desired among our belongings. Then, when he had what he wanted, the thief simply locked the door behind him and put the key back in the mailbox for "safe-keeping."

Looking back on the incident, I see that is exactly what Satan does when we have shame hidden in our hearts. He knows where the key is hidden, and he takes it out to steal from us at opportune times. He wants to rob us of our peace, our purpose, and our perspective. As long as that key is hidden, he knows exactly where to look.

There's only one solution. Don't hide the key. Give the key to God. No more hiding. No more shame.

In *Who Holds the Key to Your Heart?* Lysa TerKeurst gives us this assurance:

> Rest assured, my friend, inside most hearts exists a secret place. Behind a door of hidden thoughts and painful memories brews a hurt so overwhelming it can't be allowed to surface. The slightest peek inside reveals insecurities better left alone. So the door is locked and secrets are kept even from God. Or are they?
>
> The truth is God knows the secrets of your heart and He wants them. The maker of this vast and wonderful universe is waiting for the key to the heart of His greatest creation—you. He wants the key to your heart, your whole heart, especially the hidden parts.

When you hold this key, Satan will wrestle it from you, unlock your shame, and use it to accuse and condemn you. He loves to keep a person in such a defeated state of mind that she becomes totally ineffective for the cause of Christ. The irony is that the very things you consider shameful can be used by God for His glory.

This is the beauty of Christ's death and resurrection. The price has been paid and your slate wiped clean. There is no sin too big to keep you from the touch of the Master's hand. God is still in the miracle business, and He wants the key to your heart.[2]

Forgiving Yourself

Shame is a strong emotion that is brought on by lack of forgiveness...from yourself for yourself. While the Holy Spirit convicts us of sin to bring us to repentance, the devil condemns us with our sins to bring us to inactivity and despair.

Audrey was a woman who had committed adultery. God had miraculously restored her marriage and covered her with grace and forgiveness. Her husband, children, and parents forgave her as well, but two years later, in a prayer meeting, she realized she had never forgiven herself. She tells about a time, after a Valentine's dinner, when a close friend prayed for her.

That Valentine's Day is marked in my heart forever. After dinner, Dr. Don began ministering to all of us. As he was praying for me, he identified acute grief that was locked up deep in my heart. He went on to explain that we all go through grief, but that this was something different. It was the result of extreme loss of something or someone, and this grief was locked inside. I looked around the room, and everyone was quiet. I then proceeded to tell the story of what had happened just two short years before. My grief was locked in because I hadn't yet forgiven myself for what took place. I was holding in the sorrow and pain and keeping it close to my heart. On the outside, few people would notice. God knew, however, and I quickly discovered that I was in the middle of yet another divine appointment.[3]

That night Audrey forgave herself and was released from her deep-seated grief. God removed her shame and she is absolutely radiant today. As the Bible says, "Those who look to him are radiant; their faces are never covered with shame" (Psalm 34:5).

Jesus said, "If the Son sets you free, you will be free indeed" (John 8:36). No ifs, ands, or buts about it. It is a done deal. God forgives us the moment we ask. However, we can continue to condemn ourselves all the way to Peter's pearly gates. But it is a false accusation—one that undoubtedly Satan, the father of lies, whispers in our ears.

The Bible says that Jesus' sacrifice cleanses "our consciences from acts that lead to death" (Hebrews 9:14), and "there is now no condemnation for those that are in Christ Jesus" (Romans 8:1). "See, I lay a stone in Zion, a chosen and precious cornerstone, and the one who trusts in him will never be put to shame" (1 Peter 2:6).

Remembering the Pain

While we must accept God's forgiveness and forgive ourselves, we never truly forget. Honestly, I'm glad. If I forgot the sins and the pain that was attached to them, then I would be more likely to make the same mistakes again. God removes the shame and the penalty, but memory helps us to never go down that path again.

Remembering our weakness also helps us to be more compassionate with others when they fall into seductive traps. I am much more merciful now than I was 30 years ago when my mistakes were fewer. Looking at others' mistakes on the backdrop of my own dark past makes them less visible to the judging eye.

I can say with John Wesley, who spoke after watching a man being hauled off to the gallows, "But by the grace of God, there go I."

The Lifter of My Head

When my son, Steven, was growing up, I could always tell when he had done something wrong. He lowered his head, walked with a bit of a slump, and refused to make eye contact with me. Yep, I could always tell that he had done something wrong...I just had to figure out what.

Every day I see men and women who walk with the same posture of defeat, fear, and shame. And yet God longs to place His finger under their chins, lift their eyes to meet His, and tell them they could be forgiven and washed clean if they would but ask. David wrote, "You are a shield around me, O Lord; you bestow glory on me and lift up my head" (Psalm 3:3).

God has a plan for your life: "'For I know the plans I have for you,' declares the Lord, 'plans to prosper you and not to harm you, plans to give you hope and a future'" (Jeremiah 29:11). Satan also has a plan: He comes to "kill and steal and destroy" (John 10:10). Amazingly, it all boils down to one question—Whom are we going to believe? The truth of God that says we are forgiven and made new or the lies of Satan that say we are condemned and not worth the dirt we're made of? I choose to believe God. I hope you do too.

NINE

Removing the Mask and Being Real

Whether he is a sinner or not, I don't know.
One thing I do know. I was blind but now I see!
JOHN 9:25

I can still remember the Saturday night ritual at my house when I was six years old. My mother wound my sun-streaked ash-blond hair in what seemed like a hundred pink sponge rollers. She'd swipe her middle and pointer fingers through the jar of blue Dippity-do, slather it on a swatch of hair, and then wind the sponge round and round. My "ouches" and winces were met with "be still" and "stop squirming."

Why did she put me through the torture and sentence me to a fitful night's sleep trying to find a comfortable spot to lay my head? Because the next day was Sunday and we were going to church lookin' good. On Sundays our family drove to church, many times fighting all the way, and walked through the pristine double doors with smiles and platitudes.

"How are you?" the fellow parishioners asked.

"Fine," we mechanically replied. "And how are you?"

"Fine, thank you."

But we were anything but fine, and I imagine that the folks on the pews beside us were anything but fine, either.

My home was riddled with unhappiness. My father drank heavily, and Saturday nights were usually the worst. My mom was extremely unhappy, I was lonely and afraid, and my brother, most of the time, was just plain mad. But nobody knew. We hid it well.

What is it about church that makes us put on masks to cover up what is really going on inside? Forget the fig leaves. We've moved on to designer clothes, shiny cars, and smiling faces in order to attend the masquerade ball we call "church."

Why do we do it? Is it because we don't want to appear weak? Is it that we want to appear as strong as the Rock of Gibraltar, even if our husband just lost his job, our son is flunking out of school, our parents are dying with cancer, and we just discovered a lump while showering that very morning?

"How are you?"

"Fine, just fine. Praise the Lord."

Sometimes church becomes our stage where we play "Let's Pretend." But as the audience applauds our performance, the Director's voice grows faintly dim.

There is a scene in C.S. Lewis' *The Lion, the Witch, and the Wardrobe* that exemplifies what I think God longs for in the body of Christ. The White Witch has turned many of the inhabitants of Narnia into stone statues. Then, in a valiant display of courage, Aslan, the lion Christlike figure, pounces into the courtyard and breathes on each of the statues...bringing them back to life. Let's join in the party for just a moment...

> The courtyard looked no longer like a museum; it looked more like a zoo. Creatures were running after

Aslan and dancing round him till he was almost hidden in the crowd. Instead of all that deadly white the courtyard was now a blaze of colors; glossy chestnut sides of centaurs, indigo horns of unicorns, dazzling plumage of birds, reddy-brown of foxes, dogs and satyrs, yellow stockings and crimson hoods of dwarfs; and the birch-girls in silver, and the beech-girls in fresh, transparent green, and the larch-girls in green so bright that it was almost yellow. And instead of the deadly silence the whole place rang with the sound of happy roarings, brayings, yelpings, barkings, squealings, cooings, neighings, stampings, shouts, hurrahs, songs and laughter.[1]

I fear that our churches have turned into the stone courtyard where everyone tries to blend in and conform to the image...not of Christ...but to what others expect from churchgoing folks. However, we were never meant to be a gathering of identical statues, but of colorful, wildly wonderful individuals...real people... unmasked.

While I was doing a book tour for *Becoming the Woman of His Dreams,* I sat in the green room of a television station with a 30-year-old unmarried pastor who was a guest for a different segment of the program.

"What are you talking about today?" he asked.

"I'm doing an interview on my book *Becoming the Woman of His Dreams,*" I replied. "I interviewed hundreds of men to come up with seven qualities every man longs for."

"Really," he replied with sudden interest. "What are they?"

"You tell me."

"Well, she needs to be a godly woman," he began. "One that can be a helpmate."

He went on for a little while and I just smiled.

"Okay, you've given me your 'church' answer," I teased. "Now tell me the truth. Tell me what you really want."

"That's right," his friend yelled from across the room. "That's not what you told me in the restaurant last night!"

We had a good chuckle, and he did end up telling me what those longings really were. But it just proved again that the masks we wear in the Christian community many times veil the truth of who we really are.

We're a Mess

At least once every Sunday, Pastor Tom Henry said these words during his sermon, "I'm a mess!" Tom is one of the most transparent pastors I have ever known. He didn't mind if we knew he struggled in his marriage, with his children, or with the elders of the church. Tom was not ashamed of his scars, and he encouraged us not to be ashamed, either.

The truth is, we are all a mess! In *Messy Spirituality*, Michael Yaconelli says, "*Messy Spirituality* is a description of the Christianity most of us live and that few of us admit. It is an attempt to break through the religious wall of secrecy and legitimize a faith which is unfinished, incomplete, and inexperienced. *Messy Spiritually* is a celebration of a discipleship which is under construction."[2]

"Our churches are filled with people who outwardly look contented and at peace but inwardly are crying out for someone to love them...just as they are—confused, frustrated, often frightened, guilty, and often unable to communicate even within their own families. But the other people in the church look so happy and contented that one seldom has the courage to admit his own deep needs before such a self-sufficient group as the average church meeting appears to be."[3]

Yaconelli sums up messy spirituality as "the refusal to pretend, to lie, or to allow others to believe we are something we are not."[4] "Unlike Quasimodo, the hunchback of Notre Dame, we need not hide all that is ugly and repulsive in us. Jesus comes not for the super-spiritual but for the wobbly and the weak-kneed who know they don't have it all together, and who are not too proud to accept the handout of amazin' grace."[5]

Carol Sittema is one of my heroes who has refused to be anything but authentic, regardless of how messy her life may seem. For a few short years, God allowed her to be a part of our church to show us what it means to be real.

Unmasked and Unveiled

We gathered in the fireplace room of the family life center to meet and greet our new associate pastor's wife, Carol. Dr. John Sittema was joining us from Dallas, Texas, and all the ladies of the church were anxious to meet his new wife. Dr. Sittema's first wife had died of cancer several years before, and he and Carol had only been married two years.

After a covered-dish dinner, Carol approached the podium to share her story.

"Thank you for having me come and share a little bit about myself tonight, but I have to warn you, this might not be the typical pastor's wife story some of you expect. Let me start at the beginning.

"When my mom was in school, she met and married what my grandparents considered a low-class boy from the wrong side of the tracks. She was enamored with this guy and quit school to be his wife. Soon after they said, 'I do,' he began drinking and beating her. After the kids came along, we began to be mom's protector.

"I can remember my mother coming in our rooms to sleep because she was afraid of my dad. On more than one occasion, my dad would do things to my mom in front of us that we should have never seen. And that was my childhood as I remember it. We scraped by, I was afraid, and I learned that sex was something dirty that needed to be avoided.

"My mom stayed with my dad for twenty years. One night, when she was seven months pregnant, he almost beat her to death. But the turning point was when he turned his violence on my brother and me when we tried to protect her. That is when she left and got a restraining order against him. I was a junior in high school and wondered why she had waited so long. We lost our house and our financial support, but at least we were safe. My mom got a job in a department store making three hundred dollars a month. We had no insurance, no child support or welfare, and lived off of beans and rice.

"I never had a childhood, really. It seemed I was born to manage. However, I did go to a program called Y-Teens at the YMCA and Girls Scouts. So I got a glimpse of what 'normal' families looked like.

"Somehow, I knew I was smart. I graduated forty-second out of seven hundred in high school and decided to go to college. It was in the sixties when the world went wild...and I was no exception. My brother, who had joined the Navy, turned us all on to pot. I became a hippie, marched for any cause that came along, and my roommate was a witch. She had powers, could predict the future, and cast spells. Strange things happened in our room. She taught me how to use Tarot cards."

(I have to stop here. I want you to imagine yourself as a fly on the wall as our new pastor's wife was telling her story. Here all the church ladies relaxed after a nice meal to hear a sweet, cleaned-up version of "Jesus Loves Me." Instead, they were aghast at total transparency and honesty. You just had to be there. Let's keep going.)

"After three years of college, I dropped out, moved into an abandoned house in Kauai, Hawaii, with my boyfriend, and worked in a cornfield. We made a woodstove out of a garbage can, bathed in a stream, and ate pineapples and bananas that grew in the fields around us.

"When working in the fields, I was drawn to a Hawaiian woman who sang praise songs to God while she worked. She talked to me about Jesus, but I told her 'that was a white man's religion' and not for me—a Hispanic woman. But she continued to talk and I continued to listen. Together we would walk down the rows of corn, pulling tassels while she told me Bible stories.

"'Come to church with me, Carol,' she said one day.

"And because I had grown to love this big Hawaiian woman, I said yes.

"I don't remember much about that day, except that I heard the gospel of Jesus Christ and cried and cried. The pastor prayed for me to receive Christ, and I did. Later, someone put a Bible in my make-shift mailbox, and every time I read it, the words seemed to jump off the page. After I had gone to church, I tried to continue using the Tarot cards my college roommate had given me, but I couldn't make them work. For the first time, I was afraid of the witchcraft I had been exposed to and dabbled in. What I didn't understand is that the light was exposing and driving away the darkness. I felt God's presence, but I wasn't sure what it was. It was like feeling someone's presence when you know he is in the room.

"Also, for the first time I felt guilt for living with my boyfriend. We ended our relationship, and I moved back to El Paso to live with my mother. Boy, now that was hard. She taunted me about my failures, and when she saw me reading my Bible she said, 'What makes you think God could forgive you?'

"I decided to go back to college and finish up. While I was there, I was still looking much the hippie—no bra, sandaled feet, halter top, unshaved legs—well, you get the picture. I was sitting with a bunch of my old friends one day, and we started talking about the book of Revelation in the Bible. A clean-cut guy came up and asked, 'What are you guys talking about?'

"We told him, and he sat down with us. He opened up the Bible and began to explain all the things we were questioning. I was amazed at how much he knew about the Bible. Later, he asked me to come to a Campus Crusade meeting. I went, feeling very out of place with all the 'church people.' But they loved and accepted me. One of the female leaders invited me to lunch, and she eventually became one of my mentors.

"Let's fast-forward here. Eventually, I graduated and went on staff with Campus Crusade. I started working with a group of minority students—Blacks, Asians, and Native Americans. A few years later, I met a young man who was a youth group leader in a Catholic church. We dated for quite some time, but it didn't work out. I was devastated and decided to move to south Texas, where the population is ninety percent Hispanic. While there, I met a man in my apartment complex. I led him to the Lord, we started dating, and one-and-a-half-years later we were married. He applied to Dallas Theological Seminary, I had a high-paying job at an accounting firm, and all was right with the world.

"Life was clipping along at a nice steady pace for us. My husband was on the board of the Crisis Pregnancy Center there and working at a church. But one night, just before he went off to a board meeting, he dropped a bombshell.

" 'Carol, when I was little, I used to dress up like a girl.'

" 'Did you like it?'

" 'Yeah, I did.'

" 'Do you still do it?'

" 'Yeah, I do.'

"And then he walked out the door to go to his meeting.

"I don't want to go into all the gory details, but over the next several months, I tried to unravel the mystery that had become my life. We lived in a nice home on a golf course, and hidden in the attic I discovered women's dresses and makeup that my husband used in his secret life. We went through counseling and therapy, but he was unwilling to face or deal with his addiction. He was in bondage, that's for sure. And, I became in bondage to my big secret.

"I went to a twelve-step program for children of alcoholics because I learned that I was drawn to needy people, and not in a good way. While there, I saw for the first time...honesty. These people were so honest about their struggles and their wounds... their scars. And you know what? I learned how to be honest too.

"Some of you are sitting here tonight wondering what in the world has come into your church. But ladies, this is real life. I am real. That's all I know to be.

"It was six long years before our divorce was final. As you can imagine, I didn't want anything to do with men or a relationship. Jesus was enough. "

"I threw myself into my work. Several years later, I went to a dinner meeting where Pastor John Sittema came and shared his testimony. He told about how he and his wife both had cancer, and while he was getting chemotherapy in one room, his wife of twenty-five years died in another. And yet, He still trusted God. He was very real. John shared about his anger with God, the hurt over his loss, and the tiredness of his soul. I wanted to get to know this man...not to marry him...just to know him.

"Actually, I asked him out. There you have it. I'm being honest again. We had little in common. He was white...I was Hispanic. He was traditional...I was, well, not traditional. He had lived a squeaky-clean life...I had lived a 'colorful' life. I'll never forget how, when I told him about my life, he sat there, all six foot five of him, and cried.

"Well, one and a half years later, we were married. And here I am.

"I am not sure this is what you all expected to hear tonight, but this is the truth. This is me, and I'm glad to be here."

What a breath of fresh air. I was just about to stand up on the table and do a dance, but I didn't think our pew-sitting church members were quite ready for that. What they were getting was someone who wasn't afraid to be real. Carol was not and is not ashamed of her scars. They have fashioned her into the beautiful woman she is today, and God is using her realness to minister to women at every turn of her life. Her scars are beautiful to God.

I think that is the beauty of the Samaritan woman that Jesus encountered at the well. She had been hiding for so long because of her messy life, but Jesus knew that in order to get well, she had to get real. Once she came face-to-face with the truth, not to mention the Truth, she was no longer ashamed or thirsty. She left her water pot by the well and went to tell the entire village about Jesus. She was no longer focused on her past, but on her future.

"Broken people are concerned with being real; they care less about what others think than about what God knows—they are willing to die to their own reputation."[6] That night, as Carol revealed her true self to us, I saw His glory shining from her face.

Paul wrote, "We, who with unveiled faces all reflect the Lord's glory, are being transformed into his likeness with ever-increasing glory, which comes from the Lord, who is the Spirit" (2 Corinthians 3:18).

I was going to stop there, but keep reading: "Therefore, since through God's mercy we have this ministry, we do not lose heart. Rather, we have renounced secret and shameful ways; we do not use deception, nor do we distort the word of God. On the contrary, by setting forth the truth plainly we commend ourselves to every man's conscience in the sight of God" (2 Corinthians 4:1-2).

We are not ashamed of our scars and things we once held in secret. No! We speak the truth plainly and show God's mercy at work within us.

The Velveteen Woman

Most of us have read or heard of a childhood classic *The Velveteen Rabbit*. Perhaps you first heard the story snuggled in your mother's lap or, like me, as an adult with a child snuggled in *your* lap. *The Velveteen Rabbit* is a treasure I discovered in motherhood rather than in my childhood. And as with many children's books, the message carries a profound truth that resonates more with adults than with kids.

The story begins with a little boy discovering a velveteen rabbit in his stocking on Christmas morning. It was the same rabbit he had previously admired in a storefront window. The boy loved the rabbit...for at least two hours, but then he was put on the nursery shelf with all the other toys. Because he was velveteen, some of the more expensive toys snubbed him. Some of the toys boasted about being fashioned as smaller models of real things, such as boats and soldiers. But the rabbit didn't even know that there was such a thing as a real rabbit. He thought all were just as he was, stuffed with sawdust. But one night, the rabbit made a fascinating discovery.

One particular toy in the nursery had outlived all the other windup mechanical toys. The Skin Horse was worn but wise. So the rabbit posed an important question.

> "What is REAL?" asked the Rabbit one day, when they were lying side by side near the nursery fender, before Nana came to tidy the room. "Does it mean having things that buzz inside you and a stick-out handle?"
>
> "Real isn't how you are made," said the Skin Horse. "It's a thing that happens to you. When a child loves you for a long, long time, not just to play with, but REALLY loves you, then you become Real."
>
> "Does it hurt?" asked the Rabbit.
>
> "Sometimes," said the Skin Horse, for he was always truthful. "When you are Real you don't mind being hurt."
>
> "Does it happen all at once, like being wound up," he asked, "or bit by bit?"
>
> "It doesn't happen all at once," said the Skin Horse. "You become. It takes a long time. That's why it doesn't often happen to people who break easily, or have sharp edges, or who have to be carefully kept. Generally, by the time you are Real, most of your hair has been loved off, and your eyes drop out and you get loose in the joints and very shabby. But these things don't matter at all, because once you are Real you can't be ugly, except to people who don't understand."[7]

The Velveteen Rabbit wasn't even sure what a rabbit was supposed to do. He just knew there had to be more to life than being filled with sawdust and sitting on a shelf.

Being real. That's what really matters. I don't want to wait until most of my hair has fallen out and I've lost my stuffing. I want to be real right now. So what if I don't look as shiny as the other toys in the nursery.

Yes, sometimes it is painful to become real. It takes courage. But until we do, we'll find our existence sitting on the shelves a dim reflection of the freedom and jubilant dance that God intended in the fields of life.

Jacob Becomes Real

Jacob—now there was a fellow who didn't know how to be real. He was the son of Isaac and the twin brother of Esau. When he was born, even though he was not the firstborn, God promised that the older (Esau) would serve the younger (Jacob). Jacob was always his mama's favorite, and she wanted to make sure he received the blessing of the firstborn. Rather than trust God to do what He said He would do, she decided to help Him out a bit. So she dressed Jacob up like his hairy brother and tricked her nearly blind husband into giving Esau's blessing to Jacob. When his younger son approached Isaac's deathbed, Isaac asked Jacob, "Are you really my son Esau?"

"I am," he lied.

So Isaac gave Jacob Esau's blessing (Genesis 27:1-29).

Later, when Jacob became marrying age, His father-in-law-to-be tricked him into marrying the weak-eyed Leah rather than the promised Rachel. Ah, but Jacob wouldn't be outdone. After all, he had learned from the best—his mom. Jacob in turn tricked his father-in-law and took the best of his livestock for himself. Jacob was a trickster, and he continued to be in control of his life...or so he thought (Genesis 30:29-31:1).

But there came a time in Jacob's life when he couldn't control his circumstances. He was heading back to his homeland to face his brother Esau...the one from whom he had stolen his birthright and inheritance. Would Esau kill him? Would Esau welcome him? Would Esau slay his family? Would Esau forgive him? All these questions and more tumbled around in Jacob's mind.

The night before he was to meet with his brother, Jacob had a close encounter of the heavenly kind. In Genesis 32:22-31 we read about his wrestling match with an angel. For years Jacob had been trying to control and manage his life on his own terms, but he knew he had no control over what was going to happen the next day when he faced Esau. All night Jacob wrestled with the angel, trying to convince the angel to bless him. But before that could happen, Jacob had to face reality.

When Jacob's father, Isaac, had asked him, "Who are you?" Jacob had pretended to be someone he was not and answered "Esau." During the wrestling match, the angel gave Jacob another chance to right that wrong.

"What is your name?" (verse 27).

This time Jacob didn't pretend to be someone he was not, but answered truthfully. "Jacob" (verse 27).

"No pretending, no trying to leave a good impression, no explaining, no justifying. Jacob spoke the bare, naked truth. 'Jacob—the schemer, the deceiver, the manipulator, the con artist. That's who I am.'"[8]

Once Jacob decided to be real and give up trying to be someone he was not, God empowered him with His strength and gave him a new name. No longer was he Jacob, "the trickster," but now he was Israel, "Prince with God." Oh yes, he walked with a limp for the rest of his life. Sometimes that's the result of being real. But that limp was a reminder to Jacob that God was in control. It was his scar.

Being Real Begets Being Real

It was the first meeting of Julie's small-group Bible study. Eight women from her church gathered in a circle to introduce themselves.

"I am so glad you could all be here today," Julie began. "We are here to study the Bible and to get to know each other. Some of us have known one another for a while, and some of us don't know each other at all, except maybe by name. So for the next few minutes, let's go around the circle and tell a little bit about how long you've been at the church and something about your family."

One by one the ladies gave glowing reports of wonderful husbands, high-achieving children, and active church lives. Then it was Amanda's turn.

There was an uncomfortable pause as Amanda's eyes filled with tears. "I'm glad you all have such wonderful lives, but mine stinks right now. My marriage is falling apart, my kids are out of control, and I am here because I feel as though I'm about to lose it."

Julie got up from her seat, walked across the room, and embraced her new *real* friend. Then the meeting started afresh. Once again, the ladies went around the circle sharing about their lives, but this time it was a different story. The masks were off and they told of their own struggles. Truth was an icebreaker that created streams of cleansing tears on streaked faces of real women sharing their hurts and hearts.

Author and counselor Brenda Waggoner explains, "To be real, to be authentic, is not always pleasant. It doesn't make sparkling light dinner conversation, and you cannot unmask all your pain with every acquaintance. But those of us who are unwilling to settle for superficial spirituality must learn to be honest with ourselves and with God. And we all need someone with skin on—be it a counselor, a pastor, or a circle of trusted friends—with whom we can open up and be vulnerable."[9]

In another children's classic, *The Wizard of Oz,* we meet a man who was the antithesis of real. While he pretended to be a wizard, in reality, his magic was simply bells, whistles, smoke, and fire. The wizard was living a lie, and people falsely respected and feared him because he appeared to be something he was not. It took a little dog pulling back a curtain to reveal the truth—an old white-haired man with nothing more than a few levers, buttons, and microphones.

Interestingly enough, when the "wizard" was exposed and the truth was revealed, he left the land of Oz and set out on the adventure of his life.

Being Real with God

It's one thing to be real with each other, but can we be real with God? We might as well; He knows our hearts better than anyone else anyway. In *The Knowledge of the Holy,* A.W. Tozer wrote,

> How unutterably sweet is the knowledge that our Heavenly Father knows us completely. No talebearer can inform on us; no enemy can make an accusation stick; no forgotten skeleton can come tumbling out of some hidden closet to abash us and expose our past; no unsuspected weakness in our characters can come to light to turn God away from us, since He knew us utterly before we knew Him and called us to Himself in the full knowledge of everything that was against us.

God knew the real me before I even knew myself. David wrote, "Before a word is on my tongue you know it completely, O LORD" (Psalm 139:4).

Jeremiah was a mighty man of God who was not afraid to be real before His maker. He wrote,

> I am the man who has seen affliction because of the rod of His wrath. He has driven me and made me walk in darkness and not in light. Surely against me He has turned His hand repeatedly all the day. He has caused my flesh and my skin to waste away. He has broken my bones. He has besieged and encompassed me with bitterness and hardship. In dark places He has made me dwell, like those who have long been dead (Lamentations 3:1-6 NASB).

Jeremiah was mad, and he was mad at God. As far as he was concerned, God was the cause of all his problems. He felt trapped and afraid. He continues,

> He has walled me in so that I cannot go out; He has made my chain heavy. Even when I cry out and call for help, He shuts out my prayer. He has blocked my ways

with hewn stone; He has made my paths crooked. He is to me like a bear lying in wait, like a lion in secret places. He has turned aside my ways and torn me to pieces; He has made me desolate...So I say, "My strength has perished, and so has my hope from the LORD" (verses 7-11,18).

Jeremiah was in a bad situation...mostly because he had a wrong perception of God. God *did not* make him to walk in darkness, cause his flesh to waste away, or break his bones. God *had not* encompassed him with bitterness or hardship. But Jeremiah had allowed his perception to be skewed by his circumstances.

Even though what Jeremiah had to say was incorrect and certainly painted an inaccurate picture of God, he was able to be real about what he was feeling. Jeremiah did not feel the need to put on a holy mask before an all-knowing God. And you know what? God didn't strike him dead for being real and saying what was on his heart.

Before we leave poor Jeremiah, let's notice what happens at the end of his lament. He begins to remember all the times that God had been faithful.

> This I recall to my mind, therefore I have hope. The LORD's lovingkindnesses indeed never cease, for His compassions never fail. They are new every morning; great is Your faithfulness. "The LORD is my portion," says my soul, "therefore I have hope in Him" (verses 21-24 NASB).

Jeremiah cleaned the clutter out of his emotional closet and rediscovered the treasures he had forgotten were there. His circumstances didn't change. God didn't change. But his attitude and perception of God changed, and his emotions followed close behind.

Throwing Away the Mask

When Steve and I lost our second child, I was devastated. I wish

I could tell you that I held my chin high, clung to the knowledge of the sovereignty of God, and quoted "All things work together for the good" to everyone who said they were sorry for my pain. But I didn't. I was mad at God. I was disappointed in Him. I went to bed, pulled the covers up over my head, and told God I'd get back with Him in a few months...or years.

It hurts to tell you that, but it's the truth.

Here's the good news. For about three months I mourned for that little girl and didn't talk to God. But you know where He was all that time? Right by my side.

"I will never leave you or forsake you," God said.

"Even if I don't want to talk to You?" I asked.

"Even then."

God created us to be naked and unashamed. Fig leaves and masks were man's idea. He knows all there is to know—even what we don't.

One of my friends was visiting his family and changing clothes in his old childhood bedroom. The family housekeeper, who had been with them for more than 30 years walked in unannounced and caught Andrew with his pants down. Embarrassed, he scrambled to cover himself.

"Mr. Duffy," she chided, "don't be embarrassed. I done seen you 'fore you done seen yourself."

We might be embarrassed because God catches us emotionally with our pants down, but child, He done seen you 'fore you done seen yourself. And you know what? He loves you just the way you are.

TEN

Resisting the Fear of Rejection

*If God is for us, who can be against us? He who
did not spare his own Son, but gave him up for us all—how will
he not also, along with him, graciously give us all things?
Who will bring any charge against those whom God has chosen?
It is God who justifies.*
ROMANS 8:31-33

I was teaching at a speaker's conference. The attendees were comprised of women who felt God calling them to the podium to speak and teach or to pen and ink to write. Two hundred and sixty women were placed in small groups of ten to "practice" their speaking skills. During our first small-group time together, the ladies had five minutes to share a prepared message. Then, on the second day, we gathered again for them to share another five-minute message.

Patty was in my group. She was a vivacious, bubbly redhead with an obvious love for the Lord. But on the second day of the seminar, I sensed a change in Patty's demeanor. As we dismissed from our small-group time, I pulled her aside.

"Patty, are you okay?"

Instantly, her amber eyes filled with tears. "I had my talk for tonight all planned out, but I think God wants me to share something different."

"That's great," I encouraged. "It is always best to share what God puts on your heart, even if it is different from your original plans. You share what God wants you to share."

"You don't understand," she said through tears that were now streaming down her cheeks. "I've made friends here. I don't want them to know my story. I don't want anyone to know my story!"

"Oh, Patty, this is a safe place," I assured her. "There is nothing you can tell us that would change our opinion of you."

"I wouldn't be so sure about that," she said.

Then for the next 30 minutes, God gave me the privilege of sitting with one of His precious children and hearing about how He had redeemed her life from the pit. She was a living, breathing, walking miracle—and nobody even knew it.

I encouraged her to tell her story. She agreed to pray about it.

That evening, our group gathered in our meeting room to deliver and critique the five-minute presentations. My assistant had her stopwatch and one-minute warning card ready.

Patty was the third woman to approach the podium. She stood, introduced herself, and then a single tear spilled down her cheek.

"What I have to share is very difficult for me," she began.

"Patty, before you begin, I'd like for us to forget the stopwatch," I interrupted. "What is about to happen in this room is much more important than any of us learning how to do a proper presentation. God's about to heal your heart."

Then, through sobs, Patty began to tell her story.

"When I was a little girl, all I wanted to do was to grow up and be a mommy and a wife. My father was a preacher and my upbringing was very strict. There was no television, no radio, no swimming with people outside of our immediate family. My parents were very religious, but they fought a lot when I was gone. One day, I found out that the man I loved more than anyone on earth had had an affair.

"My mother lost a husband and my sister and brother lost a father, but I lost the one person in the world who loved me more than any other. I was a daddy's girl, and I lost the most important person in my life.

"My family went from being incredibly close to each other to each one fending for himself. We were in survival mode, fighting a similar battle, but on individual battlefields in our hearts and minds. I didn't see my father very often, but on my sixteenth birthday, he left a present on the front porch, and I caught a glimpse of his tail-lights as he drove away. I was encouraged that he remembered my birthday, but when his lights disappeared from view, I felt the light in my own life go dim.

"Both of my parents remarried and both divorced their second spouses. Later, both married for a third time. I never shed a tear during those years but stuffed my pain into a deep, dark closet. I felt that nobody loved me, so I looked for anyone who would accept me and make me feel special. Unfortunately, I turned to another woman and entered into a homosexual relationship.

"For ten years I lived a life of homosexuality, not only as a mere participant, but as a vocal and active supporter for the coalition for gay and lesbian rights. I volunteered at a gay and lesbian help line center and counseled gays on issues they were dealing with at the time. I was the sick and hurting leading the sick and hurting. Later I was in charge of a newsletter for the gay and lesbian coalition. It was a life of absolute immorality, and yet I continued to pray and beg God not to let go of me and turn me over to my own way of thinking. I hurt my parents very badly. I even demanded that if my mom wanted to see me, she would have to let me bring whomever I was with at the time with me, which included holidays. Oh, how my mother must have loved me and the complete heartbreak this must have been for her. Being in that lifestyle is so all-consuming and such a brainwash...unless you have been there it is hard to explain. Satan twists your thinking to where you honestly, whole-heartedly believe that your friends are your true family.

"I went from one relationship to another searching for true love to mend my hurts instead of looking to God. I fed off others who were searching as well. The change of address stickers on my mail started mounting up until little yellow stickers covered the enve-lopes. As odd as it seemed, I attended a church for gays, hoping God would approve of what I was doing, even though I knew it was an abomination to Him. Oh, how faithful He was to me."

At this point Patty began to shake with sobs. I approached the podium, placed my arm around her shoulders and gently coaxed her to continue.

"I moved to another state with one of the leaders of the gay movement in the area. During one of our 'retreats,' my entire group of 'friends' turned against me and accused me of lying about a cer-tain matter. Each one turned their back on me and asked me to leave their circle. This was the final rejection. Crying uncontrol-lably, I left and headed back to my hometown. I don't remember how I got there. Amazingly, when I arrived home, I had a small spare tire on my wheel, but I don't remember having a flat or anyone changing it along the way.

"I was admitted to a counseling facility called Rapha to undergo intense treatment. I had not showered, eaten, slept, or combed my hair in days. I was unresponsive to therapy, and the staff sus-pected I would die. After a week of no change, someone came into my room and placed a book, *Search for Significance,* on my night-stand. I picked it up and began reading about my life on every page. God was speaking to me, and even though I wasn't listening to the counselors, I began to hear Him through the pages of the book. I began to cry and cry and cry, but it was a healing cry. I was on my way back.

"God had to strip me of my home, my job, and all my friends in order to save me from myself. What Satan meant for evil, God is using for good. What mercy...what grace. I am amazed that God chose to save me, bless me, and now use me in His kingdom."

What happened after Patty finished her story? Were the women in the room disgusted? Were they appalled or did they think she was horrible? Quite the contrary. Each woman in the group walked to the front of the room, and we all embraced into one tangle of hugging arms and beautiful glistening tears. Then we all praised God for Patty's story of redemption and prayed for God to use her mightily to set captives of homosexuality free.

Patty's life is a portrait of a woman who revealed the truth of her scars, and she is now helping others drop the same chains that had her bound for so long. She is a beautiful young woman with a very masculine handsome husband and two lovely children. God is using Patty to help families with prodigals living in the gay life-style and encouraging them to not lose hope.

Before Patty revealed her incredible story, I can imagine Satan's tauntings. *Don't do it! Don't do it! They will hate you! You'll be sorry! Who will want to be your friend if they know the truth?*

I am so glad she didn't listen to his lies but resisted the fear of rejection. By the way, we didn't hate her—we loved her. She's not sorry—she's free. And who wants to be her friend? I do. She is very near and dear to my heart. Her scars are beautiful to me...and they are beautiful to God.

Biblical Overcomers

We have only to flip through the pages of the Bible to see that overcoming the fear of rejection is a thread that runs through the record of history.

- Noah overcame the fear of rejection when he obeyed God and built an Ark on dry land.

- Abram overcame the fear of rejection when he left his homeland with no clear direction as to where he would go.

- Jacob overcame the fear of rejection when he returned to his homeland and his brother, whom he had deceived.

- Joseph overcame the fear of rejection when he refused Potiphar's wife's sexual advances.

- Moses overcame the fear of rejection when he went before Pharaoh and demanded the Israelites' release.

- Joshua overcame the fear of rejection when he told the army their orders were to march around Jericho in silence for seven days.

- Ruth, the Moabite, overcame her fear of rejection when she gleaned wheat in the field of a Jew.

- Samuel overcame the fear of rejection when the people decided they wanted a king rather than God to be their ruler.

- David overcame the fear of rejection when he offered to slay Goliath.

- Shadrach, Meshach, and Abednego overcame the fear of rejection when they refused to bow and worship King Nebuchadnezzar.

- Esther overcame the fear of rejection when she went before the king to plea for the lives of her people.

- Each and every one of the prophets overcame the fear of rejection as they delivered God's message of judgment to the people.

When we turn the final page of the Old Testament and look into the New Testament, we see the same pattern of courage. Jesus, His disciples, Paul, and the expanding body of believers all faced and overcame the fear of rejection. Paul's attitude was "for to me, to live is Christ and to die is gain" (Philippians 1:21). It doesn't matter what anyone thinks. "If God is for us, who can be against us?...

Who will bring any charge against those whom God has chosen? It is God who justifies" (Romans 8:31,33).

Of course, the ultimate rejection occurred when our Lord and Savior hung on a Roman cross. "He was despised and rejected by men" (Isaiah 53:3). But Jesus overcame the fear of rejection and the result was His glorification. He knew crucifixion was imminent. Just before He was arrested, Jesus prayed with His disciples: "Father, the time has come. Glorify your Son, that your Son may glorify you" (John 17:1). He didn't mention His rejection and death on the cross that was ahead of Him. He prayed that God would be glorified. That was foremost in His mind and on His heart. Likewise, I believe that we overcome the fear of rejection when glorifying God is foremost on *our* minds and in *our* hearts.

The apostle Paul faced rejection at every turn. In his first letter to the Thessalonians he wrote:

> We had previously suffered and been insulted in Philippi, as you know, but with the help of our God we dared to tell you his gospel in spite of strong opposition. For the appeal we make does not spring from error or impure motives, nor are we trying to trick you. On the contrary, we speak as men approved by God to be entrusted with the gospel. We are not trying to please men but God, who tests our hearts (1 Thessalonians 2:2-4).

Whether it is sharing the gospel or the scars of our pasts, there will be some who will not accept us. We certainly are not above the prophets in the Old Testament or the disciples in the New. Not everyone liked what they had to say, but they pressed through fear and walked in faith. It is because of them we have the gospel at our very fingertips.

A Man Who Said No

Most of the men and women in the Bible are there because they said yes to God. However, there are a few more colorful characters who made the record book because of their propensity to say no. Jonah is one of those men.

In the beginning of the book of Jonah, we read that God came to him with an assignment to preach repentance to the wicked people of Nineveh...not a very popular topic, I would imagine.

Jonah did not like this assignment one little bit. So he ran from the inevitability of rejection and hopped on a boat headed in the opposite direction...Tarshish.

But Jonah learned what many of us have learned through the years—you can't run from God. God sent a mighty wind to stir the sea and toss the sailing vessel violently. After throwing most of the cargo overboard to lighten the load, the crew wondered among themselves if the storm could possibly be judgment from an angry god.

"Who are you and where are you from?" they asked Jonah.

"I am a Hebrew and I worship the LORD, the God of heaven, who made the sea and the land" (Jonah 1:9).

"What have you done to anger your God?"

Jonah told the men that he was running from God and the storm was his fault.

"'Pick me up and throw me into the sea,' he replied, 'and it will become calm. I know that it is my fault that this great storm has come upon you'" (verse 12).

Have you ever thought that your disobedience could cause storms that affect those around you? Jonah and the crew experienced this phenomenon firsthand. While they did not want to kill an "innocent" man, they had no choice but to toss him into the sea. As soon as they did, the storm abated.

This story is a whale of a tale...only it is true. God sent a big fish to swallow Jonah and spit him up on the shore three days later. This time Jonah resisted the fear of rejection and obeyed the Lord of love. In the end, the entire city of Nineveh heeded Jonah's words from God, repented of their evil ways, and received grace and forgiveness. There's nothing like spending three days in the belly of a fish to straighten out your attitude.

A Woman Who Said Yes

I had been speaking at a women's retreat near Little Rock, Arkansas. A wonderful trio led us in praise and worship. The three women were spunky, spiritually mature, and spontaneously full of praise.

Toward of the end of the second session, I shared about not being ashamed of our scars and using our past to help others recognize the healing power of Jesus in our lives. After the close, one of the women from the worship team stood away from the group who had congregated near a wooden cross at the center of the stage, but she was close enough that I could see tears glistening in her dark brown eyes.

"Marita," I whispered as I guided her to an empty pew, "what's going on in your heart right now?"

"Sharon," she replied, "what you said about not being ashamed of our scars really spoke to me. I think that God is telling me that I have been hiding the truth way too long."

"What truth is that?"

"You see, I sing on this praise team," she explained. "I travel all around the country ministering to other people. But no one knows my story. Well, some know part of it. Most people just think I'm a nice little church lady who has lived a spotless life."

"But that's not the case?"

"No, that's not the case."

"Can you tell me about it?"

For the next several minutes, Marita unveiled a hidden story of heartbreak, betrayal, and pain.

"I've been divorced...twice. The man I'm married to now is my third husband. Most think he is my one and only.

"I was raised in Northwest Arkansas," she continued. "I grew up in the church and my parents were rock-solid Christians. When I went away to college, I met a wonderful young man who treated me like a princess. We were in a Bible college and sang in a Christian music group together. I'll admit, I wasn't head over heels in love with him, but there was nothing he wouldn't do for me. It appeared that he was the perfect match for me. When he asked me to marry him, I thought it would be foolish not to say yes. He was everything I had dreamed about.

"The day before the wedding, he said he didn't want to see me. It seemed strange to me, but I just brushed it off.

"Our wedding was like a beautiful fairy tale with my white flowing gown, men in black tuxedoes, and bridesmaids in stunning rose colored dresses. My grandfather performed the ceremony. It was perfect. But what I didn't know was that my husband's vows were a farce."

"When we reached our honeymoon destination, my husband of just a few hours turned to me and said, 'Marita, I shouldn't have married you. I don't love you and I never did. The plans were just too far along for me to break it off.'

"At first I was in shock. But as soon as I regained my senses, I began to scream and pound on his chest.

" 'How could you?' I cried. 'Why did you marry me? Why didn't you call it off? What am I supposed to do?'

"The rest of the honeymoon is a blur. I was a broken woman.

"The marriage didn't last very long. We did not return to college; instead, my husband took a job as a music minister of a church. Over the next twelve months, he changed jobs several times and depended on me to support our little family. It wasn't long before we were signing divorce papers and I was once again living with my parents.

"I was twenty years old and divorced—something I didn't think would ever happen to me. Anger and bitterness became my constant companions. I felt as though I had lived a life that would please God and even married the sort of man that He would approve of. And this was my reward?

"During that time, there was a man at work who befriended me. He was ten years older than me and financially able to shower me with gifts. His attention pulled me from my dark place, and his promise of a bright future gave me hope. A year after my divorce, I married once again.

"Life was good...for a while. But then husband number two was arrested for embezzlement. The prosecuting attorney required him to move out of the area or face criminal charges. So I packed up all our belongings and we moved two hours away from our hometown.

"After he was arrested, Don started drinking heavily. One night, my greatest fear became a reality and he beat me black-and-blue. A neighbor heard the yelling and screaming and called the police. I didn't press charges. Sharon, from there it just got worse. The night he pointed a gun at me was the night I left.

"Even though we both went to counseling after that incident, he would not agree to stop drinking. Finally, I filed for divorce.

"For the next year, I slept.

"I moved back in with my parents, and for the next twelve months I went to work and went to bed. That was my existence. I am sure that my parents were very embarrassed and ashamed, but they never let on. They were wonderful and loved me through all my ugly trials."

"Marita," I asked, "how old were you at this time?"

"I was twenty-five."

"Well, I know you have a wonderful husband now. How did that come about?"

"Daryl and I had gone to first through sixth grades together," Marita continued. "A friend at his church told him that I had moved back to town. He said that he had loved me since I was twelve years old, but I don't know about that."

For the first time, I saw the twinkle of a smile dance in Marita's eyes. I knew there was a happy ending on the way.

"Daryl and I dated for eighteen months, and he asked me to marry him several times, but I was wrapped tight in fear. I had failed twice! Finally, one day I said yes. We have been married for twenty-five years and have two precious sons, one twenty-two and one sixteen."

"So, Marita, now that you've told me your story, what do you think God wants you to do with it?" I asked.

"I'm not sure," she replied, "but I don't think He wants me to hide it any longer. Most people don't even know I've been divorced once, let alone twice. But I am starting to see that God could use my story. There are so many hurting women in this church, and I think that I can show them that there is hope.

"All my life, I've worried about what people think. Not only that, I've worried about what they might think of God if they knew He had allowed me to have such heartbreak. I guess I've been trying to protect us both."

After our talk, I encouraged Marita to pray about what God would have her do with her story of redemption. Several months later I heard from her again.

"Well, Sharon," said Marita's perky voice on the other end of the phone line. "I told my story tonight."

"Really? What happened?"

"I mentor a group of young married women, and we are studying the book *Every Woman's Battle.* In the book there is a story about a woman letting go of the past and embracing victory. Rather than reading the woman's story, I told them another one. At the end, I told them that the woman in the story was me. The women were so moved. One said, 'I can't believe how much you love the Lord and how positive you are all the time. It is amazing that you could have suffered so much pain and yet keep that smile on your face and in your heart.'

"I told her a forgiving God put it there."

"How do you feel?" I asked.

"Free."

I have kept in touch with Marita to hear of how God is using her to restore marriages and mend broken hearts. She is not worried about being rejected by those in her sphere of influence—she is accepted by God.

God is using her. God is using her scars. She is thankful beyond words.

The Alabaster Box

Marita is thankful beyond words...that's why she sings. The woman who washed Jesus' feet with her tears would relate to that (Luke 7:36-50). I can just picture her pushing through the crowds on the dusty streets of Capernaum. "Have you seen Him? Have you seen Him?" she asks. "I heard that Jesus was in town. Do you know where He is?"

"Yes," someone sneers, "but what would He want with the likes of you?"

"Where is He?" she begs. "Please tell me. Where is He?"

"He is having dinner at Simon's house, but you'll not be welcomed there."

The woman picks up the corners of her robe and runs to the familiar house of the Pharisee. She bursts through the wooden door and her eyes are transfixed on Jesus, her Savior, reclining at the table. Men stare at her. Some know her by reputation; some because they have been paying customers.

Slowly, ignoring the jeers of the men gathered round, she walks over to Jesus—her eyes never leaving His. Gingerly, she kneels before Him, and takes His feet in her hands. Tears begin to drop from her eyes like raindrops. Then streamlets of tears cut through the caked-on mud and dust of His feet. Scandalously she pulls the pins from her raven hair, and it cascades over her shoulders and back. She takes the tresses and gently dries Jesus' feet. All the while, tears of gratitude and worship stream down her weathered cheeks as she covers her Savior's feet with kisses.

A hush fills the room as the woman who had lived a sinful life reveals an alabaster jar of perfume and pours its contents on her beloved Master's feet. The fragrance of grace fills the room and clings to the unsuspecting crowd.

This woman had many scars, but she was no longer ashamed. She was free! How precious that God chose to use *her* to minister to His Son. She resisted the fear of rejection and worshipped her Lord.

ELEVEN

Rejecting the Lie of Disqualification

When you have turned back, strengthen your brothers.
LUKE 22:31

From the time I heard my son's first cry, I knew that I was about to embark on one of the most incredible journeys of my life—and I was right. Being a mom has been the most fulfilling, frustrating, exciting, exhausting, mind-boggling, hair-raising, thrilling, tiring, stimulating, soul-stirring, delightful, difficult, consuming, laborious, uplifting, inspiring, challenging, captivating, and rewarding job I've ever had. When Steven was born, I had no idea how much love could be wrapped in one tiny package. Over the years, Steven has pulled on my heartstrings like an angel plucking the strings of a golden harp to fill the heavenlies with beautiful music.

However, not all days were so melodious. Sometimes I felt as

163

though those heartstrings were being plucked by a little devil's pitchfork. I've questioned my parenting, doubted my abilities, and wondered if I should be disqualified from a ministry that encourages and equips moms to raise the next generation for Christ.

When Steven was born, I became a student of motherhood. I observed mothers who did it well, listened to what grown children had to say about what their mothers did right and not so right, read history books to see what mothers of successful men and women did to instill godly values, studied the Bible for God's wisdom, and prayed fervently for God to make the best of my mistakes.

Steven was in the ninth grade when I turned in my manuscript for *Being a Great Mom, Raising Great Kids*. The book was a culmination of years of research, study, and experience. At the time, I was President of Proverbs 31 Ministries, an international radio, magazine, online, and speaking ministry to bring God's peace, perspective, and purpose to today's busy woman. Steven was a great kid. I felt like a great mom. All was right with the world.

However, the day after I tied up the neatly typed pages and slipped them into the mailbox headed for the publisher's office, my world was rocked on its axis.

The phone rang.

"Hey, Mom, this is Steven."

"What are you doing calling in the middle of the day?" I asked. "Is everything okay?"

"No," he said. "I'm in the principal's office. I've been caught stealing."

I don't really remember what happened next. All I know is that I found myself sitting in the principal's office wondering who that boy was sitting there wearing my son's clothes. The principal sat behind his desk as Steven stared at his shoes and confessed to his mom.

"For several weeks," he began, "I took bags of chips from the lunchroom during break. I didn't pay for them. I just took them."

"Why did you do that?"

"I don't know. I guess it became a game to see if I could do it and not get caught."

At that moment I felt like anything BUT a great mom and I felt that Steven was anything BUT a great kid. He got a week of in-school suspension and I got a month of house arrest. It wasn't that I couldn't leave the house, but I sure didn't want to.

Doubt, confusion, anger, insecurity, uncertainty, grief, and embarrassment kept me locked up. *Who was I to be telling anyone about how to be a parent? Who was I to be running an international ministry? Who was I to be speaking in front of thousands of women each year? Who was I to be doing an international radio feature?*

I felt that I had to resign from my position and my ministry because I was...*disqualified.*

What Qualifies Us to Be Disqualified?

Some of you may be thinking, *Boy, that's nothing! So what if your son stole from the school cafeteria? I've stolen from my place of employment. I've sold my body for cash. I've snorted crack cocaine. I've had an abortion. I've lied to my husband. I cheated in college. I...*

We can fall into a trap comparing scars and trying to decide whose is the deepest or most severe. *My pain is worse than your pain. My life was more traumatic than your life. My sin is more grievous than your sin.* Regardless of the size or severity of the scar, Satan still hisses the same lie...*disqualified.*

Maybe you don't feel that you deserve to serve the Lord because of what you've done. But guess what? You never *deserved* to serve God in the first place. None of us do. If we think that it all boils down to who deserves to serve and who does not deserve to serve, then we are placing way too much value on our part in the redemption process. It is as if we are saying we had something to do with it. Listen, sister, it is all God in the first place, and it will be all God in the last place.

While Steven's sin was the problem in this case, I can assure you my reaction to it was just as bad.

Bible teacher Beth Moore has this to say about being disqualified because of past sin:

> I will not argue that the type of service may need to change, but to refuse true servants the right to serve at all is nearly to destroy them. I would rather be that person...at the judgment than the audacious person who enforces such a death sentence on the repentant (James 2:12-13).
>
> I don't even think those who have never been wholeheartedly devoted and end up falling in their own rebellion ought to be refused the right to serve after complete repentance and an active pursuit toward spiritual wellness. Their failure may be the very thing God uses to sift them and make them true foot-washing servants.
>
> The truly repentant are often so purified and humbled by disaster that they are willing to do anything! If persons who claim repentance are still arrogant and unwilling to take responsibility, they are probably missing the fruit of repentance. They are a long way from ready. But don't bail out on them even then! Help them, speak the truth in love, and pray them to true repentance![1]

If sin disqualified us from ministry, then we would all be hiding in our houses. Just take a look at some of the men and women in the Bible. David wasn't disqualified from being God's choice as king of Israel because he committed adultery and murder. Rahab wasn't disqualified from being assimilated into the Israelite nation because of her past profession as a prostitute. Gideon wasn't disqualified from being the leader of God's army because he was hiding like a coward in a winepress. Saul (whose name God changed to Paul) wasn't disqualified from being a crusader and evangelist to the Gentiles because he had persecuted the church before his encounter with Jesus. Peter wasn't disqualified from being one of the founding fathers of the Christian church because he denied Jesus three times.

Hear me on this. If our past failures and mistakes disqualify us from ministry, then none of us would pass the test. King David wrote, "If you, O Lord, kept a record of sins, O Lord, who could stand? But with you there is forgiveness; therefore you are feared... put your hope in the Lord, for with the Lord is unfailing love and with him is full redemption" (Psalm 130:3-4,7). I couldn't find one example in the Bible where a repentant person was disqualified from future service.

Satan uses our past failures and weakness against us to make us feel disqualified. He also uses what has been done to us by others to make us feel unfit or ineligible.

Michael Yaconelli writes:

> Not everyone has chosen their past. Too many carry the scars of physical, mental, or psychological abuse, awakening each day to the haunting memories of a time when they were acted upon, against their will, and now find themselves hopelessly trapped between facing their past or running from it. A sad reality of modern life is the increasing number of people whose past abuse has convinced them of their unworthiness. Often it is the abused who have decided they are disqualified from the possibility of God's grace. The abused see themselves as damaged beyond repair, soiled goods which cannot be cleaned, prisoners who cannot be freed."[2]

Tamar was King David's daughter and Absalom's sister. And while her name meant "Palm Tree," a symbol of victory and honor, her life became a symbol of defeat and despair. One day, when Tamar least expected it, her half-brother Amnon violently raped her and then tossed her away like a filthy rag. She was a woman who felt disqualified because of what was done to her.

After the attack, Absalom cared for and protected Tamar in his own home. Eventually, he exacted revenge and killed the rapist, but she never felt like a princess ever again. For the rest of her days she lived in darkness and desolation. (Read Tamar's story in 2 Samuel 13.)

Tamar's father never did anything to restore his daughter to her rightful place. But, friend, your heavenly Father did! He sent His Son, Jesus, to remove your filthy rags and place a royal robe on your shoulders. "He [God] has sent me [Jesus] to bind up the brokenhearted, to proclaim freedom for the captives and release from darkness for the prisoners...to comfort all who mourn, and provide for those who grieve...to bestow on them a crown of beauty instead of ashes, the oil of gladness instead of mourning, and a garment of praise instead of a spirit of despair" (Isaiah 61:1-3).

Whether it is something you have done or something that was done to you, Satan will use the information and the experience to try to make you feel disqualified. However, God has said that you are qualified the moment you believed on Jesus Christ, His Son. While your scars mark you, they do not make you.

"We are God's workmanship, created in Christ Jesus to do good works, which God prepared in advance for us to do" (Ephesians 2:10). Did you catch that? He planned work for you to do before you were born. Do you think that His plans for your life could possibly be negated because of something that has happened in your past? Oh no, dear one. No plans of God's can be thwarted (Job 42:2).

God "has *qualified* you to share in the inheritance of the saints in the kingdom of light. For he has rescued us from the dominion of darkness and brought us into the kingdom of the Son he loves, in whom we have redemption, the forgiveness of sins" (Colossians 1:12-14, emphasis added). He does the qualifying. Not me. Not you. Not anyone. Only God.

Satan is a meticulous note taker when it comes to our past mistakes, but God is a miraculous sin eraser. Why, God even destroys the list!

Rahab Saves the Day

Several years ago, I traveled to the Christian Booksellers Association convention in New Orleans, Louisiana. Why the committee chose New Orleans, I will never know, but I must say I got quite an education while I was there.

One afternoon I decided to go exploring down the famous Bourbon Street. It seemed there was some sort of street party going on. Before I knew it, I was shoulder to shoulder in a mass of humanity—a herd of hoopin' and hollerin,' dancin' and drinkin' carousers. I kept my purse pressed to my chest and looked for the next exit! Bombarded by a cacophony of sights, sounds, and smells, my eyes traveled up to a balcony overhead. Even though it was broad daylight, several "ladies of the evening" were hanging over the railing enticing the men below to join them for sensual plea- sure—by the hour.

The "ladies" wore bustiers, thigh-high hose with feathery garter belts, and lacy push-up camisoles. With six-inch heels on their feet, dangling jewels from their earlobes, and vibrantly painted lips, they hung over the balcony of what appeared to be a brothel, displaying their bodies with alluring words to seduce their prey.

Never having seen a brothel before, I now had a better picture of what Rahab's house in the Bible must have looked like. In the Old Testament, just before the Israelites conquered, captured, and claimed the Promised Land, they sent in spies to check out Jeri- cho's defenses. While there, they went into the house of a prosti- tute, probably because no one would be suspicious of strange men entering there. The officials made an official visit in search of the spies, but Rahab hid them under stalks of flax until it was safe for them to leave. Before the sun rose the following morning, Rahab made a statement of faith:

> I know that the LORD has given this land to you and that a great fear of you has fallen on us, so that all who live in this country are melting in fear because of you. We have heard how the LORD dried up the water of the Red Sea for you when you came out of Egypt, and what you did to Sihon and Og, the two kings of the Amor- ites east of the Jordan, whom you completely destroyed. When we heard of it, our hearts melted and everyone's

> courage failed because of you, for the LORD your God is God in heaven above and on the earth below. Now then, please swear to me by the LORD that you will show kindness to my family, because I have shown kindness to you (Joshua 2:9-12).

The spies told Rahab to tie a scarlet cord in her window and bring her entire family into the house. When the army came to destroy the city, they looked for the scarlet cord and rescued Rahab and her family.

I get so excited about this story. We have a scarlet cord as well! It is Jesus Christ, God's only Son, whose scarlet blood saves us, protects us, and delivers us. You know what is so wonderful? Rahab wasn't only saved from destruction, but she was brought into the family of God and used for His glory. She even married a wonderful Jewish man named Salmon. Perhaps you haven't heard of him, but I bet you've heard of their son, Boaz, or their grandson, Obed, or their great-grandson, Jesse, or their great-great-grandson, David.

No matter what we've done or where we've come from, when we come to Christ and tie that scarlet cord from the window of our heart, God saves us, welcomes us, and uses us for His glory. Unfortunately, many people believe they are forgiven, but they don't feel that they are good enough to be used. They stand like an outsider, like a waif peering into the window of a great mansion as a banquet is taking place within. Their tummies grumble in hunger as the father slices the roast turkey and the juices seep over the braised meat. Their mouths water as the rich gravy smothers the steamy potatoes and the sweet biscuits are passed from person to person.

But what they fail to see is the empty seat—the one with their name printed on the place card.

You have been brought into God's family and invited to dine at your Father's banqueting table. Don't stare through the window. Go in and take your seat where you belong. He's waiting for you.

"She [Rahab] lives among the Israelites to this day" (Joshua 6:25).

Strategic Maneuvers

Did you catch the timing of Steven's offense at the beginning of this chapter? I fully believe it was not an accident that he ended up in the principal's office the day after I turned in my manuscript for a parenting book. I can imagine Satan planning and scheming all along.

"Okay, boys," he must have said, "let's tempt Sharon's son to do something wrong, something really bad. We'll let him get by with it for a few weeks, but then, just as she mails that disgusting book on raising godly kids, we'll let him get caught. That will devastate her! She'll quit all this ministry stuff, stop talking about Jesus all the time, and keep her mouth shut! Now, go get her!"

"But what about the boy?" one of the demons might have asked.

"I don't care about him. He's just the cannon fodder we're using to get at her. That's her weakest spot. We'll get at her by getting to her kid."

Does that make you mad? It makes me mad.

Like an expert manipulator, Satan's timing is always impeccable. Just like the Japanese, who bombed Pearl Harbor on a lazy Sunday morning in December 1941, our enemy tries to catch us off guard when we least expect it.

We probably all remember the account of Jesus fasting and praying in the desert for 40 days before He began His three years of ministry on earth. When Jesus was at His physically weakest point, Satan, the opportunist, tempted him with food and power. Jesus fought back with a powerful sword of his own—the Word of God. After Satan conceded defeat, he slinked off to wait a while. The Bible says this: "When the devil had finished all this tempting, he left him until *an opportune time*" (Luke 4:13, emphasis added). He said, "I'll be back!"

Understand this. Satan's goal is to stop us, shut us up, and shut us down. He is the one who tells us we are disqualified because of our scars. However, God tells us that in our weakness we are made strong.

A Call to a Friend

As I mentioned earlier in this chapter, when Steven was suspended from school, I struggled with whether I should resign from the ministry where I served. This was not a decision I could make on my own, and I felt I needed some godly counsel. I called Rod, the pastor of the youth and their parents (student families), and explained the situation.

"Rod, I feel as though I should resign," I explained. "Who am I to be telling people how to raise children?"

"Sharon," he began, "let me tell you a story. One night about 12:30 AM, I got a call—the kind that makes you feel sick in the pit of your stomach. It was a friend from church telling me that our oldest son and three of his friends were surrounded by police and about to get arrested for destruction of private property.

"I immediately drove to the scene. I was met with four police cruisers, flashing lights, and four boys cuffed and hunched in the back of the police cars. The police explained that the boys, on a dare, had jumped the curb and driven their Jeep up the steep hill of the swim club. The tires left deep ruts in the grounds. A neighbor called the police and insisted that they press charges.

"So here I was, the youth pastor of one of our city's largest churches, with four of my high school students, one being my son, cuffed and booked. The other parents and I tried to convince the police not to press charges, but they didn't have a choice. If the neighbor wanted to press charges, they had to follow through.

"The four boys were taken down to the station, fingerprinted, and photographed. They were placed in a cell until they were released to their parents' custody. They made a public apology to the neighborhood committee, wrote a letter of apology, restored the grounds to its original condition, and put in hours of community service time.

"Like you," Rod continued, "I wondered if I should resign from my position in ministry. I was very visible in the community, and I was the youth pastor for these boys—a role model. My family was supposed to be in order."

"That's exactly how I feel," I said.

"I went to our senior pastor," Rod continued. "I explained the situation and asked if I should resign. He said 'definitely not,' and that he would pray for our family. I suspect his experience raising three teenagers of his own came into play with that advice.

"While I didn't protect my son from the consequences, I didn't abandon him, either. I even went with the boys and supervised when they restored the property."

Rod helped me so much that day. He was not ashamed of his scars, and he helped me to see that a child making a mistake does not disqualify the parent from ministry...nor does it disqualify the child.

Rod mentioned three things that popped into his mind as he stood with the police lights flashing around him that evening: his reputation, his son's reputation, and Christ's reputation. Interestingly, those are the three areas that I see Satan attacking each of us to make us feel disqualified. But you know what...his tactics are always filled with lies to freeze us into inactivity. I suggest we stand beside the light of Christ, allow the warmth of His love to thaw out the ice, and begin flowing in the ministry that He has called and equipped us to do.

The Boy Who Had No Legs

It was the third game of the year for the varsity football team of Colonel White High in Dayton, Ohio. After the Colonel White team left the locker room at halftime, the refs approached the coaches on the sideline. Crew Chief Dennis Daly announced, "Number 99 cannot play in this game anymore. He's not wearing shoes, knee pads, or thigh pads."

"But he doesn't have any legs!" Coach Earl White exclaimed.

"Sorry," Daley said. "It's the rule."

Sportswriter, Rick Reilly told the story of Bobby Martin in a *Sports Illustrated* article, "Half the Size, Twice the Man." Bobby Martin was the backup noseguard and a starter on punt coverage. Bobby Martin is a kid born with no legs. But what he lacks in legs, he makes up for in courage. Bobby runs on his hands just about as quickly as his teammates do on their feet. He benches 215 in the weight room, and he hopes to try out for the track team throwing the shot put.

As Bobby sat on the bench he said, "The ref could look at me and see I don't have feet or knees. How can I wear shoes if I don't have feet?"

"A rule is a rule," the ref said.

Reilly wrote, "How can you throw a legless kid out of a game for not wearing shoes? Can you throw an armless kid out for not wearing wristbands? And even if he were suddenly to produce shoes and knee and thigh pads, where was Bobby supposed to wear them? From his ears?

"Is there anything worse than a whistle-worshiping, self-important stiff who can't see past his precious rule book to the situation that stands in front of him? Even if that 'situation' is a kid who stands about three feet tall and weighs 112 pounds, 101 of that heart?"

Reilly also quoted a radio talk show host who agreed with the ref. "The rule says you have to wear shoes and pads, period," the host said. "He can't play. He's handicapped. There's certain things handicapped people can't and shouldn't do, and one of them is play football."

Coach White tried to explain to the refs that Bobby had passed his physical and already had clearance to play from his doctors. But the referees kept saying, "We can show you the rule."

But by the next week's game, Coach White had secured a letter from the Ohio High School Athletic Association that said the officials were wrong and Bobby could resume play.[3]

Let's go back to Reilly's question: "Is there anything worse than a whistle-worshiping, self-important stiff who can't see past his precious rule book to the situation that stands in front of him?" I don't know about you, but I've seen some whistle-worshiping, self-important stiff-necked religious folks who can't see past their own precious rule book to notice a repentant, broken, redeemed child of God who stands in front of them. There will be religious refs who try to keep a repentant sinner off the field. There will be modern day Pharisees who would rather see the likes of Tamar stay in the dark and out of the public eye.

But, friends, God does not call us to the game of life to sit on the bench. He calls us to get in the game! And for those refs who would try to tell us we're disqualified? Our coach has a letter in His pocket. The Creator of the Universe says we've passed physical and spiritual tests, and we are qualified to play.

TWELVE

Revealing the Truth

We, who with unveiled faces all reflect the Lord's glory,
are being transformed into his likeness with ever-increasing glory,
which comes from the Lord, who is the Spirit.
2 CORINTHIANS 3:18

We never dreamed it would ever happen to us. Never in our wildest imagination did we think it possible. Why would we? We had everything going for us. We had it all: a "perfect" marriage, three beautiful kids, a fruitful and fulfilling television ministry, and above all else, a deep love for Jesus. Life for us was an exciting journey filled with purpose and joy. Our course was set and our way seemed sure. The forecast: calm seas ahead. Infidelity was not even a cloud on the horizon, not even the remotest glimmer in our spirit. Or so we thought. Unknown to us, it was already headed our way,

177

sweeping in low beneath our radar, ready to launch a sneak attack and catch us unawares—Audrey

Audrey and Bob had a great marriage and a growing ministry. She had been raised in a godly home with God-fearing parents. A lifetime of Christian upbringing had given Audry strong convictions and provided a stability she took for granted. They had been married for 16 years and had three wonderful children. But something happened that shook their *perfect* world forever. "I should have seen it coming," Audrey said, "but I didn't. My confidence in my own immunity is the very thing that left me completely vulnerable to infection. My pride in having an 'exceptional' marriage blinded my perception."

It all began very gradually like a small cloud forming in the distance. Audrey met a man who showered her with attention, admiration, and lavish expressions of appreciation. After a while, Audrey became addicted to the compliments and affirmation. Once the door to her heart was opened and the "hook" was in, sin drew her slowly but surely off the path of righteousness and onto a false trail of lies and self-deception. She made one small compromise, then another, and another, smugly confident that she could handle her secret world.

What began as "innocent" flirtation grew into an emotional affair. And it wasn't too long before the emotional foreplay manifested itself into a physical affair. Audrey thought she knew the enemy's voice, but somehow she succumbed to his enticing lies. "It's no big deal," Satan hissed. And before she knew it, she plunged into the deep black waters of self-deception and adultery.

"I never knew true pain," Audrey explained, "until the day I confessed my adultery and confronted the shocked reaction of the person I loved the most. The tidal wave of disbelief, horror, and anger threatened to completely envelop and choke the life out of me. In that moment, I began to know pain—Bob's as well as my own—and came to the first glimmer of understanding the magnitude of my sin."

When Audrey confessed her adultery to Bob, he responded with shock, disbelief, and horror. His seemingly perfect life began to crumble at his feet.

"I knew that what I had done was wrong," Audrey admitted. "That's why I had confessed to Bob. If I had kept silent, no one would have known—except me and God. But I needed to be free; I wanted to be free. Confession was my only option. Coming clean about my sin was the only way out of the deadly detour I had taken."

How did Bob feel? Let's let him tell us.

"When Audrey told me she had committed adultery, it was like a blow to the stomach. My first, instantaneous response was disbelief: *No this can't be happening. I can't have heard her right. I must have misunderstood her; surely she didn't say what I think she said.* As the reality hit home—as I realized deep in my gut that it was *true*—I was completely devastated. How could this have happened? What had Audrey done to me? To us? To our marriage? To our children? To our future? All of a sudden, the bottom fell out of my life. Nothing made sense anymore. The whole scenario was like a scene from some surrealistic movie. As the questions arose, so did my anger. I needed to do something, and fast, but I didn't know what. Finally, I simply walked out of the room, leaving Audrey alone with the bombshell she had dropped right into the middle of our marriage. I needed time to be alone and do—what?"

Bob could have left Audrey and never looked back. But something inside of him rose up to fight for his marriage. Immediately they sought godly counsel and began to put the broken pieces of their lives back together. It was excruciatingly painful—like handling broken pieces of glass with cutting edges. The repercussion of Audrey's sin catapulted her headlong into an "arena of death and destruction"[1] and it was going to take a miracle-working God to pull her out.

During the healing process, Bob and Audrey committed to pray with each other every day. We've all heard the statistics that one in two marriages in America (50 percent) end in divorce, even among those who attend church regularly. But here is a little known fact: According to a Gallup poll, for Christian couples who pray together daily, the divorce rate drops to one out of every 1152—that's .011 percent.[2]

Bob and Audrey's journey to healing and wholeness was not an easy one. Along the way they had to cope with a pregnancy as a result of her adultery, three moves, and the struggles of their children who traveled on this journey with them. They faced public scorn from other Christians, the accusations of being disqualified from ministry, and condemnation from those who could not accept God's grace and forgiveness extended toward them. But they decided they were not going to hide their struggle.

Bob and Audrey appeared on the television program founded by her father, *It's a New Day*. It was a very sober moment for this couple, but they flung the door of their greatest hurt wide open for the world to see. Yes, there were mixed emotions. Most rejoiced in what God had done to bring Audrey to a place of repentance, Bob to a place of forgiveness, and their marriage to a place of restoration and healing. But just as the older brother did not welcome his prodigal brother home, some did not accept Bob and Audrey. There were those who felt Audrey was disqualified from ever serving God again. Others were jealous that they could be happy after such trauma. And then there were some who felt that Audrey did not deserve to be forgiven and restored.

Like I said earlier, big brother was not happy when the prodigal returned home. He was invited to the party, but he refused to come.

Was going public and exposing their scars worth it? They would say a resounding yes!

I failed to mention when and where I met Bob and Audrey. We were sharing a shuttle on our way to a television interview where they were going to share their story of redemption and restoration. I call it *God's New Scarlet Letter...F for Forgiveness*. Their story is a testimony of hope to others that they can survive adultery or other major relationship struggles.

Today, Bob and Audrey Meisner travel around the country speaking at marriage conferences and watching God restore marriage after marriage. Their family is healthy and intact. They help answer tough questions such as: How do you rekindle lost love? How do you save a marriage devastated by infidelity and betrayal? How do you protect a marriage from the determined attack of an implacable enemy? How can a marriage not only survive but thrive in a culture of quiet desperation that hasn't a clue to the nature of true love?

They can tell men and women about tapping into true love at its supernatural source, not because they read about it in a book, but because they have been to the pit of despair and back. They have experienced the pain of infidelity and the healing touch of the One who is always faithful. (More about Bob and Audrey's story can be found in their book, *Marriage Undercover.*)

Revealing the Truth

One day I was flipping through my local newspaper and noticed a calendar of events for the week. For the first time, I perused the list to see what was happening in my fair city. Then a stark reality hit me, and I began to count. In that one week, 146 support group meetings were scheduled. There was everything from Alcoholics Anonymous to Codependents Anonymous to Recovery from Food Addiction. Then over to the side a note read, "If you're looking for a support group not listed here, call..." Once again I was struck with how desperately people need encouragement and support, and how they will go just about anywhere to get it. Unfortunately, people are seeking help outside the church because so few of us are willing to admit we have or have had a problem.

In order to reveal a scar we must put pride aside, take off the mask, and become real. The process involves dying to our own selfish pride that convinces us to appear happier, healthier, or holier than we really are. Jesus said, "Unless a grain of wheat is buried in the ground, dead to the world, it is never any more than a grain of wheat. But if it is buried, it sprouts and reproduces itself many times over. In the same way, anyone who holds onto life just as it is destroys that life. But if you let it go, reckless in your love, you'll have it forever, real and eternal" (John 12:24-25 MSG). When we take the seed of our testimony and plant it into the soil of another's wounded heart, it will bring in a harvest of healing for those who need it most—those wounded souls who feel as though they are the only ones who have experienced such failure or pain.

In *Brokenness—The Heart God Revives,* Nancy Leigh DeMoss says this about the grain: "I can take a grain of wheat and clean it up, put it on a beautiful piece of china on my dining room table, shine lights on it, play music for it, pray for it, and what will happen to it? Absolutely nothing! It will always just sit there 'alone.' What has to happen to that grain if it is to bear fruit? It must go down into the ground and die...Then—after it has 'died'—it will put down roots, and the first shoots of new life will finally spring forth."[3]

She goes on to say, "With all our talk of worship, unity, reconciliation, love, and the power of God, we have bypassed the essential ingredient that makes these things possible. I believe a return to this truth—the need for brokenness and humility—is the starting place for experiencing the revival we so desperately need in our lives, our homes, and our churches."[4]

When we reveal the truth that has been hidden like a treasure beneath the soil, there will be some who will scoff and scorn. And unfortunately, many of those will be Bible-toting church members—"religious power brokers."[5]

When We Keep Silent

What happens to us when we keep silent about the pain of our past? One thing is for sure, it doesn't disappear. Listen to what King David said about his silence: "When I kept silent, my bones wasted away through my groaning all day long. For day and night your hand was heavy upon me; my strength was sapped as in the heat of summer. Then I acknowledged my sin to you and did not cover up my iniquity. I said, 'I will confess my transgressions to the LORD'—and you forgave the guilt of my sin" (Psalm 32:3-5).

Studies have actually shown that telling a secret, whether to a friend, a loved one, or a virtual stranger, can be good for your health. "Self-disclosure has repeatedly been found to boost one's immune system and reduce shame and guilt," says James W. Pennebaker, PhD, a psychologist and the author of *Opening Up.*[6] There is even a website to which people can mail their secrets on postcards and have them posted anonymously.

When we are truly repentant, humbled and broken, we don't mind who knows about our scars because we have nothing to lose. And those who hear our stories of redemption have everything to gain. Brennan Manning wrote, "To live by grace means to acknowledge my whole life story, the light side and the dark. In admitting my shadow side I learn who I am and what God's grace means."[7]

There is one note of caution here. While confession is "good for the soul," as many have said, it does not mean that we should go around saying whatever we want to whomever we want. Though after emotionally erupting you may be able to say "I'm glad I got that off my chest," you may have placed a heavy burden on someone else. Be careful about what and with whom you share.

The Look of Love

So often at women's retreats, I am approached by women racked with the pain of shame and defeat. Their invisible cloak of shame is so heavy that it drags on the ground behind them and weighs them down. Words such as "If you only knew," "I could never tell anyone," "What I did was so horrible," and "I'm such a fake" are commonplace. And even though the wound occurred many years in the past, to them it was but just a moment ago.

Gina was one such woman. She was absolutely adorable. She had a petite frame with chocolate eyes, a beautiful smile, and perky bobbed hair. But as we stood under the cross at the end of the main session, a session where we nailed our burdens and past mistakes to a wooden cross, I saw that those big brown eyes were red from tears and that a cloak of shame was puddled at her feet.

"Gina, do you want to talk about it?" I asked as others cleared the room.

"I can't," she cried. "I am so ashamed."

"Do you want to tell me?"

"Yes," she continued. "I want to tell someone. I want to tell you, but I'm afraid. I've never told anyone."

"Come on outside," I said as I led her to two rocking chairs overlooking the Great Smoky Mountains.

For the next hour or so, Gina poured out her story.

When she was in high school, her mother remarried. It wasn't too long afterward that her stepfather began to make sexual advances toward her. Gina's mother either didn't see what was happening or refused to admit the truth. Gina felt her only recourse was to escape—so she ran away from home. No money. No safe harbor. No anchor. No friends.

"I didn't have anywhere to go," she said. "I didn't have enough money to even rent an apartment. But then I met this woman who seemed to care about me. She told me about a way to make money, more money than I could ever make working at a minimum wage job. Even though I was repulsed at first, she told me that I'd get used to it in no time at all."

"What did she want you to do?" I asked, fearing the worst.

"Prostitution," she sobbed.

"I didn't get used to it," she continued. "And every time I did it, a part of me died. I didn't do it for long, just a few times, but I've never been able to forget the shame and how dirty I felt. Even though I'm now married, have two children, and a wonderful life, I still feel dirty. It was a long time ago, but it feels like yesterday. Nobody knows. My husband doesn't know. He always tells me how precious I am. If he knew, it would kill him."

We talked for a long time about God's forgiveness, how Jesus didn't condemn the woman caught in adultery but forgave her and told her to walk away from her life of sin, and about what

God actually offered us at the cross—a clean slate. Gina knew most of that in her head, but it was her heart that was having trouble believing it could be so easy.

After we talked I asked, "Are you glad you told me?"

"Yes," she said. "Mainly because the way you are looking at me now is not any different than the way that you were looking at me before you knew."

Oh, dear one, that is the same way it is with Jesus. He looks at us with the same love after the fact as before. And I believe that we will be surprised how many others will look at us with that same love and compassion when we reveal our scars of the past. It is Satan who tells us that we will be condemned because he doesn't want us to be free.

There may be some pious souls who judge us or condemn us, but you know what? It just doesn't matter. "Who will bring any charge against those whom God has chosen? It is God who justifies" (Romans 8:33). Sister, you are already justified, sanctified, and purified. Now all you need to do is believe God for the power and get fortified!

Here's how Jesus deals with those with a condemning spirit:

> Jesus went to the Mount of Olives. At dawn he appeared again in the temple courts, where all the people gathered around him, and he sat down to teach them. The teachers of the law and the Pharisees brought in a woman caught in adultery. They made her stand before the group and said to Jesus, "Teacher, this woman was caught in the act of adultery. In the Law Moses commanded us to stone such women. Now what do you say?" They were using this question as a trap, in order to have a basis for accusing him. But Jesus bent down and started to write on the ground with his finger. When they kept on questioning him, he straightened up and said to them, "If any one of you is without sin, let him be the first to throw a stone at her." Again he stooped down and wrote on the ground. At this, those who heard

began to go away one at a time, the older ones first, until only Jesus was left, with the woman still standing there. Jesus straightened up and asked her, "Woman, where are they? Has no one condemned you?" "No one, sir," she said. "Then neither do I condemn you," Jesus declared. "Go now and leave your life of sin" (John 8:1-11).

A Woman Tells All

Remember the woman at the well? She was a gal who went from hiding her scars to wearing them like a neon sign that flashed FORGIVEN! FORGIVEN! Let's go to the well and recall her story.

After Jesus had spent some time ministering in Judea, He decided to go back to His hometown of Galilee. Most respectable Jews would cross the Jordan River and travel along the east side of the banks to avoid the despicable country of Samaria. The Samaritans were half-breeds who had intermarried with Gentiles, and the Jews didn't want anything to do with them. However, Jesus "had to go" (John 4:4) through Samaria, not because of geography, but because His Father had sent Him on a divine appointment.

Jesus had traveled ahead of His disciples and reached Jacob's well while the Twelve went into town to purchase some food. Tired and thirsty, He sat down by the well's edge. After a few moments, a Samaritan woman came to draw her water for the day. Traditionally, the village women came to draw water early in the morning or at the end of the day to avoid the heat of the sun. However, this particular woman did not want to associate with the other women, or at least they did not want to associate with her. She was tired of the piercing stares, the hissing whispers, and the cutting sideways glances cast her way. For her, the scorching sun was easier to endure than the scorn of the villagers. So she came to the well at noon. She was ashamed of her scars...and rightly so.

As she prepared to dip her bucket into the well, Jesus asked, "Will you give me a drink?" (John 4:7).

The woman was shocked that Jesus would make such a request.

"You are a Jew and I am a Samaritan woman. How can you ask me for a drink?" (verse 9).

It wasn't unusual for a thirsty traveler to ask for a cool drink of water, but it was scandalous for a Jewish man to carry on a public conversation with a woman, especially a Samaritan woman. It was unheard of for a Jewish rabbi to drink from the same cup as a Samaritan, male or female.

Her reply to Jesus most likely had a hint of sarcasm, but Jesus did not let that deter His mission. He was more interested in winning the woman than winning the argument. "Jesus answered her, 'If you knew the gift of God and who it is that asks you for a drink, you would have asked him and he would have given you living water...Everyone who drinks this water will be thirsty again, but whoever drinks the water I give him will never thirst. Indeed, the water I give him will become in him a spring of water welling up to eternal life'" (verses 10,13-14).

Living water. Never thirst again. Just the thought of never having to come to the well and face the whispers of the townspeople again was enough to pique her interest. But Jesus had more for this woman than water for her parched body—He had satisfaction for her parched soul.

> The woman said to Him, "Sir, give me this water so that I won't get thirsty and have to keep coming here to draw water." He told her, "Go call your husband and come back." "I have no husband," she replied. Jesus said to her, "You are right when you say you have no husband. The fact is you have had five husbands, and the man you now have is not your husband. What you have just said is quite true" (John 4:15-18).

Jesus talked to her as though she mattered. She did.

The Light of the World had revealed her innermost darkness. She was amazed that Jesus saw right through her as if He had seen every day of her life. She believed Him when He said He was the Messiah. All her life she had been seeking fulfillment. She had gone from one man to the next, but her heart remained as empty as the water pot she carried in her arms. However, on this day she met the only One who could satisfy her every longing. She ran into town in broad daylight, telling everyone about the man who told her everything she ever did (verse 29). No longer was she ashamed of her scars, but she put them on display and brought an entire village to Christ.

As Margaret Lee Runbeck once said, "There is no power on earth more formidable than the truth." That would apply to Jesus, who is *the Truth,* and to us when we reveal the truth.

Begin with One

Perhaps there are some parts of your life that you feel God is calling you to share. Where do you start? May I make a suggestion? Start with a few trusted friends—friends who love you—no matter what.

God never intended for us to go through life alone. As we have already seen, when He created man, He said, "It is not good for the man to be alone" (Genesis 2:18). Likewise, it is not good for any one of us to experience life alone. We need each other. Since God first created man and woman, He intended us to live in community with one another and with Him.

There is a comical scene in the movie *Crocodile Dundee.* He is at a party in New York City with his new friend Sue. She introduces Dundee to a psychiatrist, and Dundee is confused about the doctor's role.

"Don't you have psychiatrists in Australia?" Sue asks.

"No," he answered. "We just have mates" (Australian term for "friends").

As women, relationships come naturally, so let's take advantage of our God-given ability to foster relationships and share our secret hurts and healing. In an article by Melissa Healy, she notes:

> Women are keepers of each other's secrets, boosters
> of one another's wavering confidence, co-conspirators

in life's adventures. Through laughter, tears and an inexhaustible river of talk, they keep each other well, and make each other better. Now the power of girlfriends is beginning to yield its secrets to science. For women, friendship not only rules, it protects. It buffers the hardships of life's transitions; it lowers blood pressure, boosts immunity and promotes healing. It may help explain one of the medical science mysteries: why women, on average have lower rates of heart disease and longer life expectancies than men...

To be sure, friendships—the feeling of being connected to a supportive network—profoundly affect the health of both genders, according to researchers. Men and women who report loneliness die earlier, get sick more often and weather transitions with greater physical wear and tear than those who say they have a support network of friends or family."[8]

Healy quotes 82-year-old Suzanne Dragge: "With women, you can bare your soul. You don't do that with your husband, and they don't do that with you." She and her friend Connie Smith, 85, have counted church offerings, kidded each other, and fly-fished together for almost a decade. "Thank goodness for lady friends," says Suzanne.[9]

Just as God placed Ruth with Naomi, Mary with Elizabeth, and Jonathan with David, He gives us friends with whom to share our lives. It is not good for man or woman to be alone.

When I look back over some of my greatest disappointments in life, sharing them with a trusted friend helped lighten the load and gave me a godly perspective hidden by my cloud of tears. When I have shared some of my scars and shortcomings, it is in the eyes of a nonjudgmental friend where I see the reflection of Christ's compassion and love.

Someone I love very dearly was sucked into the seduction of sexual sin. I wanted to be a friend with whom she could bear her soul. During a lunch I was that safe place for her to expose her wound and hopefully begin the healing process to possessing a beautiful scar.

A few days after our meeting, she wrote me a note. I share this with you not to pat myself on the back, but to show you that by being a safe place for someone to heal, you are Christ's representative in a very unforgiving world:

> Dear, dear Sharon
>
> On Wednesday I was privileged to have lunch with Christ Himself. His very being, spirit, love, and character supped with me and listened to my starving, impoverished soul and said, "I love you—unconditionally. There is NOTHING you could ever do to cause me to reject you as my treasured friend."
>
> I joined Him broken, poured out, and needy. I left Him fed, nourished, and fortified in His truth, and loved with a love I will NEVER forget.
>
> Sharon, I give God high praise for His residence in you, His love that exudes, and His truth that is honest, forthright, and unchanging. Oh, dear servant of our Lord Jesus Christ, this child of His thanks Him for you.
>
> I love you.

Do you have such a friend who will love you no matter what? Do you have someone with whom you can be totally honest? Perhaps you do, but you've never given transparency a try. If you have hidden your scars in the deep recesses of your heart, and yet they are bursting to be released, I encourage you to tell your story.

"When we go through life grasping, clinging, clutching and desperately trying to hang on to things that should naturally be released, we ache. We get tied up in knots. We become emotionally constricted and locked up in pain. We lose freedom of movement in our lives and feel paralyzed."[10]

C.S. Lewis once said, "Our whole being by its very nature is one vast need; incomplete, preparatory, empty yet cluttered, crying out for Him who can untie things that are now knotted together and tie up things that are still dangling loose." Many times, God uses the medium of friends to paint the beauty of scars on the palette of our lives. They can bring out the shades, the coloring, and the hues that we seem to have forgotten were even there.

Honestly

Sheila Walsh was a familiar face to those who watched Christian television. She was a popular recording artist and cohost of the *700 Club.* But during her tenure at the *700 Club,* something went wrong. Sheila began to lose focus and forget her questions during interviews. Sheila faced the truth that she was struggling with severe clinical depression, checked herself into a psychiatric hospital in Washington, DC, and learned how to be real.

While she was in the hospital, Sheila went to a church service where the pastor put words to her struggle.

"There are some of you here today," he began, "who feel like dead people. It is as if you are already six feet under, staring up at the top of your own locked coffin. This morning Jesus wants to set you free. You simply have to let go of the key and pass it through the little hole, where you see a tiny shaft of light."[11]

Sheila discovered many new truths about her true identity during those days and weeks in the hospital. Mainly, she was not defined by her past, but by a loving God who called her His child. But was she ready to reveal her scars to the audience who had watched her for so long? Yes, she was.

Sheila came back to the *700 Club* one more time, only this time she was not the interviewer, but the interviewee. There was some debate as to whether Sheila should tell viewers about her stay in the psychiatric hospital and struggle with depression, but she responded, "That was the simple truth, and I needed to keep telling the truth as best I could."

She did tell her story with cohosts Pat Robertson, Ben Kinchlow, and Terry Meeuwsen at her side. In the months that followed, Sheila received and read more than 5000 letters from viewers telling her about their own stories. She was amazed by letter after letter filled with stories of people struggling with their own depression or that of a loved one. Sheila was not and is not ashamed of her scars, and God is using them to bring peace and purpose to others with scars of their own.

In *Honestly,* Sheila encourages us to step out from the shadows and face the truth:

> When you step out from the shadows into the storm, you may be at the mercy of the wind for a while, but Christ is Lord over the wind and the storms, and you will be truly alive—not just a whisper of who God called you to be. There is so much more to life than mere survival! God wants you to live, not just get through one more day. We can try in vain to fix ourselves, but only the one who made us knows the path to healing.[12]

Get Ready to Fly

It can be difficult to reveal our scars, especially if they have been hidden under years and years of pretend. But a boat was not meant for the harbor, an eagle was not meant for the barn, and a bird was not meant to remain an egg. And you, my friend, were not meant to be a treasure that remains hidden in the sand.

In *Mere Christianity,* C.S. Lewis notes:

> It may be hard for an egg to turn into a bird: it would be a jolly sight harder for it to learn to fly while remaining an egg. We are like eggs at present. And you cannot go on indefinitely being just an ordinary, decent egg. We must be hatched or go bad.[13]

When you decide to reveal the truth and use the scars of your past to be a blessing to others, you will not be alone. God will be right there with you as you take one believing step after another.

Respecting the Lives of Others

Before we begin the journey of revealing the truth and using our scars to bring the message of healing to others, there is one important filter through which our stories must flow—love. "Do everything in love," Paul tells us in 1 Corinthians 16:14. So let's "take a knee" as a football coach would say, and listen up.

Let's go back to the message of chapter 2 for just a moment. "Remember, the story of our lives is not a stand-alone volume." There is no part of our story that does not affect or involve someone else. We live in community and in relationship with other human beings. In the Bible we are told to "respect" others (Leviticus 19:3; 1 Peter 2:17; 3:15). God would not have us "minister" at someone else's expense. If the motive is not love, then it does not glorify God.

For example, there is much about my past that I share and there is much in my past that I do not share. Not because I am ashamed, but because it would dishonor someone else. What I *do* share about my childhood, my mother has read and approved. But again, there are other facets and struggles that I *do not* make public because the information would hurt someone deeply.

In many of my books women and men have shared slices of their lives in order to encourage, equip, and empower others. Often I change the person's name; again, not because they are ashamed, but because sharing the particulars of someone's name (a parent, for example), would be dishonoring.

Noah's Three Sons

It wasn't too long after God created man that He grew very frustrated. "The LORD saw how great man's wickedness on the earth had become, and that every inclination of the thoughts of his heart was only evil all the time. The LORD was grieved that he had made man on the earth and his heart was filled with pain" (Genesis 6:5-6).

So God decided to wipe mankind from the face of the earth

through a great flood. The only ones He spared were Noah and his wife; their three sons: Shem, Ham, and Japheth; and their wives.

After 40 days and nights of rain and then 354 days of waiting for the waters to recede, God gave the signal for the small band of survivors to exit the ark. Their mission was to spread out, populate, and subdue the earth.

One of the first things Noah did was plant a vineyard. One day he celebrated the fruits of his labor with a bit too much of the fruit of his vineyard. Noah got drunk and passed out in his tent...naked. Ham walked in the tent, saw his father lying there naked, and then ran out to tell his brothers.

"Hey, guys," he might have said, "come over here and look at Dad. He's passed out drunk and naked as the day he was born!"

While Ham made fun of his dad and exposed his sin, the other two brothers tiptoed in and covered him up. In order to not show dishonor to their dad, the twosome covered their shoulders with a garment and walked in the tent backward so they would not see their dad and embarrass him even further. Then they gingerly placed the covering over his nakedness (Genesis 6:20-23).

When Noah woke from his stupor and found out how his youngest son had exposed and broadcasted his nakedness, Noah cursed the boy and his descendants. However, Noah blessed his other two sons (Genesis 6:24-27).

Moses came down from Mount Sinai with what we have come to know as the Ten Commandments. Sandwiched right between "keep the Sabbath day holy" and "do not murder" is the fifth commandment: "Honor your father and mother, so that you may live long in the land the LORD your God is giving you" (Exodus 20:12). Paul reminds us that this is the first commandment with a promise (Ephesians 6:2).

Dr. Neil Anderson has counseled many men and women and led them through the steps to forgiveness. The first step he asks them to do is to write down the names of the persons who have offended them. "Of the hundreds of people who have completed this list in my counseling office," Dr. Anderson said, "95 percent put father and mother as number one and two. Three out of the first four names on most lists are close relatives."[14]

It is not uncommon for the scars of our past to be inflicted by family members. That is all the more reason to respect the lives of others when sharing our stories.

Bible teacher Beth Moore often mentions the fact that she was victimized as a child. However, she has remained very general, never mentioning the perpetrator's name. "My victimization wasn't constant because my victimizer didn't have continual access to me," Beth said in an interview with *Today's Christian Woman*. "But it certainly was enough to mess me up at a time when I was figuring out who I was."[15]

When telling our story, we do not have to tell all the details, especially those that would expose another's sin.

You might be interested to know that each time I tell someone's story in a published book, I print out what I have written, send it to the person about whom I have written, and have them give me permission to share it. Sometimes we go back into a story and pull certain details out. Most times what we remove are elements that would hurt a fmily member.

Again, Paul exhorts us: "Do everything in love" (1 Corinthians 16:14). If we expose someone else's sin for our personal gain, and do so with even a hint of bitterness or anger, then we should not call that ministry.

"Show proper respect to everyone," Peter said (1 Peter 2:17). If you are going to tell your story in a public way, make sure you respect the lives of others and let love always be your guiding principle. Anything else, and it has the scent of revenge.

With that said, let's get on to the business of revealing the truth, not being ashamed of our scars, and sharing the hope and healing of Jesus Christ.

THIRTEEN

Releasing the Power of Our Scars

*They overcame him by the blood of the Lamb
and by the word of their testimony.*
REVELATION 12:11

The headline read: "Blemish for Navy Officer—Murder Charge in Orlando Shooting."

Jason Kent crewed on the U.S. Naval Academy's offshore sailing team. His love for water was supposed to take him this week to the Pacific Ocean and his first duty as an officer aboard a ship anchored in Honolulu. But the young lieutenant might never again go to sea. He spends his days in the Orange County Jail awaiting trial on a first degree murder charge.

An officer and a gentleman, Kent won't say a word about the burst of gunfire that killed his wife's ex-husband.[1]

197

Carol and Gene Kent epitomize the radiant Christian life. Carol had dedicated her life to loving her husband, raising a godly son, and leading women in how to speak up with confidence about their relationship with Jesus Christ through Speak Up with Confidence seminars.

Their son, Jason (also known as J.P.), was every mother's dream. In Carol's words, he was a "focused, disciplined, compassionate, dynamic, encouraging young man who wanted to live for things that mattered, a young adult who had dedicated himself to serving his God and his country through military service in the U.S. Navy."[2]

Jason Kent loved people. He had a stellar record in high school, lettered in sports, and was president of the National Honor Society. In addition to volunteering with Habitat for Humanity, he mentored young students and gave blood every time the Red Cross was in need. Jason earned a black belt in karate and was a leader in his church youth group. Jason was a joy to raise. He never caused trouble or gave his parents any reason for concern with inappropriate behavior. As a student in the United States Naval Academy at Annapolis, Maryland, he studied hard and earned good grades. He was disciplined, both physically and mentally, and dreamed of becoming a Navy SEAL.

But on October 23, 1999, something snapped in this young man's mind, and Carol and Gene's world was forever changed. J.P. pulled the trigger of a gun and killed a man in a grocery store parking lot.

What happened in Jason's mind? No one knows for sure. When Jason married a woman who had been married before, he received two wonderful stepdaughters. There were allegations of abuse, and several months before the shooting, Jason discovered that the biological father of the girls was seeking unsupervised visitation. Jason felt he had to protect the girls.

Carol and Gene were devastated. They questioned their parenting and their relationship with God. Their entire world was shaken, and they felt that no part of their lives was on solid ground. Carol felt "lost at sea in a tidal wave of fear and despair."[3]

In *When I Lay My Isaac Down,* Carol takes us on her four-year journey that began with receiving the phone call telling of Jason's arrest, to sitting through the trial that gave her only son a lifetime sentence in jail with no parole, to the present day of putting the pieces of their shattered lives back together. In the end, Carol and Gene realized that they had to lay their Isaac down.

"Laying our Isaac down is the hardest decision we will ever have to make. It feels risky, awkward, impractical, frightening, and ridiculous. But our hearts know it's the right thing to do. We bow in worship before the God who loves us more than we love our Isaac and open our fists. And in the process of releasing, we find ourselves deeply loved."[4]

Carol came to a crossroads in her ministry and career, as well as in her personal life. She was an international speaker. What was she to do with her ministry? Could she go on? Should she give up?

Carol reminds us, "One of the Enemy's most damaging tactics is to paralyze us with our own emotional psychological wounds—to fill us with such pain and shame that we despair of ever being able to 'get up and walk.'"[5] Carol and Gene did get up and walk. It wasn't easy to fight giving in to depression and despair, to face the extreme losses, and to decide to follow Christ no matter what. Every day they continue to relinquish their control over the outcome of their son's life—they lay their Isaac down. And the Kents have discovered the power of their scars.

Carol explains:

> There is a common ground of understanding, forgiveness, acceptance, and healing when we are authentic with each other. When we tell our real-life stories of what we have encountered on the journey of life, we break down barriers and create safe places to risk revealing the truth. Intimacy in our relationships springs to life when we are no longer hiding behind the mask of denial, embarrassment, guilt, or shame. We're just us—people who have

had some good days in life and people who have had some very bad days. We've quit pretending that everything is "fine" and that life is grand. When we share our stories with each other, we find a way of relating without the facade and without the need to impress. We can just be real. This brings tremendous freedom...

I used to wonder how any good could come out of reviewing the details and reliving the pain of an unwanted experience. But I've discovered that tremendous power is released when we dare to speak up and communicate our personal stories with honesty and vulnerability. By doing so we remind others that life is an unpredictable journey for all of us. Bad things happen, and the Enemy tries to destroy our spirit and our sense of purpose. If we can remember that we are engaged in a spiritual battle—not with weapons and hatred, but with hope, faith, and joy—we affirm our ultimate security in God and our love for Him in the midst of our heartache. The grace-filled reward is that we find ourselves enveloped in steadfast, intimate, extravagant love that continues to move us into the heart of the greatest adventure of all."[6]

Carol and Gene Kent continue to run Speak Up Speaker Services, but they have a new passion as well...Speak Up for Hope, a nonprofit organization that seeks to speak up for those that have no voice in our country's prisons. They have discovered and released the power of their scars to give hope to the hopeless, encouragement and strength to the weary, healing to marriages that have been torn apart by incarceration, and mental, spiritual, and physical stability to the children of prisoners.

God's Economy

What do you think of when you hear the word "power"? Webster defines "power" as "an ability or faculty, control, controlling influence, authority." In the Greek, the original language of the

New Testament, the word is *dunamis* and means "that which manifests God's power."[7] It is where we get the English word "dynamite."

In the Bible, Jesus told the disciples that they would receive power after He had died and the Holy Spirit came to live in and through them (Acts 1:8). "It is for your good that I am going away. Unless I go away, the Counselor will not come to you; but if I go, I will send him to you" (John 16:7). In the disciples' minds, that did not make sense. Why would it be better for Jesus to leave them? How could they possibly have more power if He were gone?

That certainly would not have been the way the disciples would have planned Jesus' reign. Even Peter, when Jesus foretold of his imminent suffering, death, and resurrection said, "Never, Lord! This shall never happen to you!" (Mark 16:22).

They did not understand God's economy: the first shall be last, we gain our lives by dying to self, we receive by giving, we become powerful by being weak, we are lifted up when we humble ourselves before God.

In Jesus' first recorded sermon, He began with a list of seeming contradictions.

> Blessed are the poor in spirit,
>   for theirs is the kingdom of heaven.
> Blessed are those who mourn,
>   for they will be comforted.
> Blessed are the meek,
>   for they will inherit the earth (Matthew 5:3-5).

In *Brokenness—The Heart God Revives,* Nancy Leigh DeMoss notes the following concerning Jesus' words about the poor in spirit:

> Jesus came to introduce a radically different way of thinking about life. In the Greek language in which the New Testament was originally written, there are two words Jesus could have chosen to speak of someone being "poor." The first word suggests someone who

lives just below the poverty line, someone who is always having to scrimp and scrape to survive, someone who makes it, but barely. That is not the word Jesus chose. He used another word that means a beggar—a person who is utterly, absolutely destitute. This beggar has no hope of surviving unless somebody reaches out a hand and pulls him up.

What is Jesus saying? Blessed are the beggars—those who recognize that they are spiritually destitute and bankrupt. They know that they have no chance of survival apart from God's intervening mercy and grace.[8]

Consider these seemingly upside-down verses from Scripture:

- Whoever wants to become *great* among you must be your *servant,* and whoever wants to be *first* must be your *slave*— just as the Son of Man did not come to be served, but to serve, and to give his life as a ransom for many (Matthew 20:26-28, emphasis added).

- *Give,* and it will be *given to you.* A good measure, pressed down, shaken together and running over, it will be poured into your lap. For with the measure you use, it will be measured to you (Luke 6:38, emphasis added).

- Then he said to them, "Whoever welcomes this little child in my name welcomes me; and whoever welcomes me welcomes the one who sent me. For he who is *least* among you all—he is the *greatest*" (Luke 9:48, emphasis added).

- But God chose the foolish things of the world to shame the wise; God chose the weak things of the world to shame the strong. He chose the lowly things of this world and the despised things—and the things that are not—to nullify the things that are, so that no one may boast before him (1 Corinthians 1:27-29).

- But he said to me, "My grace is sufficient for you, for my *power* is made perfect in *weakness.*" Therefore I will boast all the more gladly about my weaknesses, so that Christ's power may rest on me (2 Corinthians 12:9, emphasis added).

- *Humble* yourselves before the Lord, and he will *lift you up* (James 4:10, emphasis added).

We tend to think that our scars hinder our service for God when it is often our very scars that render us able. Through our weakness, He makes us strong. Through our dying, He makes us alive. Through our wounds, He makes us whole. It is in the telling and showing that God's power is released.

Going Full Circle

In the Old Testament book of Exodus, we find God's chosen people serving as slaves to the mighty Egyptians. Because the Hebrews had grown so numerous, Pharaoh decided to make all Hebrews serve the Egyptian people as slaves in hopes of subduing them. For 400 years the Hebrew people served under the whip of the Egyptians, until one day God heard their cry and chose to set them free.

The Israelites, or Hebrews, witnessed God perform many miracles on their behalf: the river of blood, the stench of frogs, the swarm of gnats, the itch of fleas, the death of livestock, the pain of boils, the storm of hail, the destruction of locusts, the blanket of darkness, and the death of the firstborn—but these plagues that God inflicted upon the Egyptians did not touch His chosen ones. They marveled as God parted the Red Sea so they could walk across the bottom of the sea on dry land, stood amazed as God rained down manna from heaven, and rejoiced as God brought water from a rock to quench their thirst. For two years God provided for their every need.

But when it came time to enter into the Promised Land, the Israelites had a bout with doubt. Moses sent in 12 spies to check out the place—to see if it really was a land flowing with milk and honey. Upon their return, they gave the following report.

"We went into the land to which you sent us, and it does flow with milk and honey! Here is its fruit. But the people who live there are powerful, and the cities fortified and very large...We seemed like grasshoppers in our own eyes, and we looked the same to them" (Numbers 13:27-28,33).

But not all the spies were in agreement. Two men, Joshua and Caleb, assured the people that God had already given them the Promised Land. All they had to do was march in and take what was already theirs.

Unfortunately, the people believed the evil report of the ten spies rather than the promises of God. Because of their unbelief, God punished the people and did not allow that entire generation to enter the Promised Land. And even though the Hebrews were free from slavery, they lived the rest of their days wandering in the wilderness of unbelief. Unfortunately, that is where many Christians live today—saved from the penalty of sin, but wandering in the wilderness because of unbelief.

It wasn't until years later, once that entire generation of unbelieving Hebrews died off, that God gave their children another chance to enter the Promised Land. Only two men of the original generation, Joshua and Caleb, were allowed to enter. This time, the new generation of Hebrews chose to believe that God would do what He said He would do.

Their first stop, just before going into the Promised Land was a place called Gilgal, just west of the Jordan River. The word "Gilgal" means "circle." God had brought His chosen people full circle. They could finally put Egypt behind them and move into the land God had promised all along. Their parents' unbelief kept them out, but their own belief would take them in.

Many times, before moving into our Promised Land, God will take us full circle. What has wounded us is often the very thing He uses to take us to our Promised Land of ministry. When we are not ashamed of our scars, God takes us to our own personal Gilgal and leads us into a land flowing with opportunity.

An emotionally healed abuse victim works at a battered women's shelter offering hope.

A woman who knows the healing and forgiveness from a past abortion ministers to women at a crisis pregnancy center offering right choices.

An ex-drug addict reaches out to women strung out on cocaine and offers freedom.

An ex-prostitute helps women trying to break the chains of sexual sin and offers a life of purity.

A mother who has lost a child comforts other mothers who bear the fresh wounds of similar loss and grief.

A victim of rape counsels a woman ravaged by sexual violence.

There is only one person who can keep you from entering your Promised Land—you. Not the person who hurt you, abused you, neglected you, or abandoned you. Just you. God brings us full circle and asks, "Are you ready to enter into your Promised Land now?" I love this quote by Samuel Chadwick: "It is a wonder what God can do with a broken heart, if He gets all the pieces."

Coming Toe to Toe with Hope

When Melissa was born, her parents were overjoyed to welcome their firstborn baby girl into the world. However, when the doctor pointed out that two of her toes on each foot were webbed together, her mother's tears of joy were mixed with tears of apprehension.

"Don't worry," the doctor said, "ducks have webbed feet, and they get along just fine."

"But my baby girl is not a duck!" Melissa's mother cried.

Melissa doesn't remember much about growing up with her toes fused together. But when she was seven years old, she was barefoot on the playground when a little boy pointed at her feet and said, "Ewww" for all to hear. From that time forward, Melissa never allowed anyone to see her feet again.

"I kept my deformity hidden from sight," Melissa told me. "No one saw them. If someone did get a glimpse, the response was always the same...*ewwww.*"

At times Melissa felt like a freak in a circus sideshow. If someone caught a glimpse of her deformity, their exclamations would cause others to gather around. "Can I touch it?" they would say. "What does it feel like?" others would ask. It was just easier to keep the toes out of sight.

As Melissa grew into a beautiful young woman, she continued to keep her flaw hidden from the public eye. She wasn't comfortable with anyone seeing it except her husband.

When each of Melissa's four children were born, she counted each one's toes to make sure they were all there and accounted for...separately. Not surprisingly, her first child, Blake, also had two toes fused together on each foot, and many of Melissa's insecurities surfaced as she held her precious child.

Several years later, Melissa had her third child, Dylan. All of Dylan's toes were accounted for separately, but he had a different anomaly. Just below the soft spot on his head, Dylan had an unusual mass of tissue about the size of a silver dollar. The surface was bumpy, bulbous, and covered with tiny unattractive nodules.

"What is this spot on Dylan's head?" Melissa asked.

"It is called cutis aplasia," the doctor replied. "It's like scar tissue."

"Will hair ever grow to cover it up?"

"No, it won't."

"What can we do about it?"

"I suggest that you have a plastic surgeon rotate the scalp and remove the tissue. He will be left with a small scar that will resemble a part in his hair."

Melissa and her husband decided that plastic surgery would be a wonderful option...one that Dylan would thank them for years down the road.

Now, dear friends, here's the good part.

Melissa is one of my friends who is also a speaker. Just recently, she traveled to speak at a women's event in Valley Forge, Pennsylvania. The theme was Extreme Makeover: Soul Edition. During one of Melissa's sessions, she felt compelled to talk about her fused toes.

"We all have things about us that we are ashamed of," she began. Before she delved into the hidden secrets of the heart, Melissa told about her fused toes and Dylan's cutis aplasia.

As Melissa was talking, she made eye contact with a woman who looked as though she was just about to jump out of her chair. As she continued to talk, this woman's face began to glow. Melissa knew that something she said had spoken to this woman's heart. After the session, this woman was the first to run up to Melissa.

"You won't believe this," the woman exclaimed. "I also have two fused toes on each foot. I have never known anyone with fused toes, and I've hidden it all my life. As you began to talk about your feet, God began to lift the shame right off of me. I will not be embarrassed again!"

Then the two ladies sat right there on the floor, took off their shoes and compared toes. Others who gathered around could only laugh with the barefoot wonders.

When the giggling crowd dispersed, another woman, a mother of four, approached Melissa.

"You won't believe this," the young mother said, "but I was also born with cutis aplasia. I've never met anyone in my whole life who had it besides me."

Then the woman explained that two of her four children also had cutis aplasia. She and her husband were now in the process of deciding about surgery to correct their scalps.

"You probably don't know why you were sent here," the woman explained, "but I do. God sent you here just for me. I have been struggling, trying to figure out what to do with my children. People are very free with advice, but in my heart I always think, *But you don't understand.* God sent you here this weekend because

He wanted me to hear from someone who does. And in a way, He is telling me that most of all, He understands."

"Thank you for sharing your story with us," she continued with tears in her eyes. "You could have kept those flaws to yourself. But God used them to bring me hope."

"Thank you for letting me know," Melissa said. "God does love you so much. He brought me hundreds of miles just for you."

"By the way," the woman said through her smile and tearstained face, "My daughter also has fused toes."

I have chills just thinking about it. Of all the people God could have chosen to speak to that group of women in Pennsylvania, He chose Melissa. Because she was not ashamed of the flaws, deformities, and abnormalities in her life, lives were changed. From the top of her son's head to the toes of her webbed feet, God used every bit of Melissa to bring the hope and healing of Jesus Christ to these precious women.

Oh, how I love this verse: "May the God of hope fill you with all joy and peace as you trust in him, so that you may overflow with hope by the power of the Holy Spirit" (Romans 15:13). He is the God of hope! When we trust Him with our scars, our hope overflows onto those around us and gets them sopping wet with hope themselves. That's the power of our scars.

The King's Kids

The angels were hovering low in our church on this particular Sunday morning. It was a special day for a group of ten "kids" known as the King's Kids. They were leading worship by singing a special song—only many of the kids couldn't carry a tune, walk on their own, or even control their limbs. We sat in silence as the unlikely band of worship leaders stumbled onto the stage. Each of these children of God had a visible handicap. The Kids lined up on the stage, many with adults standing behind them to support them, both physically and emotionally. Kristen, a young lady with

Down syndrome, appeared to be the leader. She stood out in front of the others with confidence and strength and passion.

The sound track began and the King's Kids began to "sing" with their hands in sign language. "Press on," their hands proclaimed. With wide sweeping motions and uninhibited praise, Kristen sang with arms and hands to the One who loved her most.

There was one girl in particular who caught my eye. She was not able to do the signs by herself. Her limbs were much too weak and uncontrolled. I watched as this gal leaned into a woman standing behind her and surrendered her arms and hands. While the others signed the words to the song, the woman moved her young charge's hands in tandem with the others. Beth simply leaned into her helper and relinquished control.

Then God spoke to my heart. *That is what I want you to do. Lean into Me, relinquish control, and allow Me to move your life in a symphony of worship.*

We all have disabilities. While the handicaps vary, God longs for each one of us to do as Beth did on that Sunday morning. Lean into Him, relinquish control, and allow God to move us to His song.

Scars? We've all got them. It's how we view them that will change our hearts. It's what we choose to do with them that can change the world.

There was not a dry eye in the 2000-seat sanctuary. These precious Kids had many wounds and scars in their young lives, but they encouraged each of *us* to "press on." Their disabilities were visible, yet those of us who sat in the pews had disabilities that were not visible to the naked eye but just as real.

Are there beautiful scars in your life that need to be revealed? I wonder what God wants to accomplish through you. I wonder how long He's been waiting for you to remove the covering. Don't be ashamed of your scars, for it is by those very scars that the world will recognize the Savior, Healer, and Lord.

This is not a conclusion, my friend. It is a commission. It is not the end of our journey together, but just the beginning. Jesus said,

"Go into all the world and preach the good news to all creation" (Mark 16:15). Your *world* might be your neighborhood. It might be the other side of the globe. But wherever God leads, I pray that you will not be ashamed of your scars but reveal the truth of God's healing, redeeming, restoring power in your life. Your scars are beautiful to God.

Bible Study Guide

Lesson One—Scars Tell a Story

1. Just for fun, write down the scars you have on your body. Beside each one, write a brief story about how you got the scar and what you learned from each incident. If you are doing this Bible study in a group, pick one of your stories and share with the group.

2. Scars tell a story and indicate that healing has taken place. Read John 9 and answer the following questions:

   a. Why was the man born blind?

   b. What was the healed man's testimony when he was brought before the Pharisees?

   c. What was the power of his story? Were they able to dispute it?

   d. What did Jesus do when He heard about how the man was treated in the courts?

   e. Who did the man say that Jesus was in verse 9:38?

   f. If you were brought before a court of law to tell about why you believe in Jesus, what would be your testimony? Did healing take place? Was there a wound that is now a scar? Did He open your eyes? What happened in your life that is irrefutable proof, not secondhand knowledge from what someone told you, but first-hand knowledge because of what happened to you?

Lesson Two—Recognizing Jesus Through Our Scars

1. Read the following and note what Jesus taught His disciples about His death and resurrection:

   a. Matthew 16:21

   b. Matthew 20:17-18

   c. Mark 8:31

   d. Mark 10:32-34

2. While Jesus had explained His imminent death and resurrection to His disciples, they did not understand it or perhaps did not believe it. Now let's fast-forward to the day of His resurrection. Read Luke 24:1-12.

   a. Describe the scene.

   b. What did the women see?

   c. What did the angels say?

   d. How did the disciples respond to the news?

e. What was in Peter's mind after he had seen the empty tomb?

f. Describe how you would have felt if you had been in Peter's sandals.

3. Let's look at two other men who were confused. Continue reading in Luke 24:13-35.

a. To whom did Jesus appear?

b. Why didn't they recognize Him?

c. Considering their words in verses 21-24, you would think the men would be full of hope, and yet they were downcast and discouraged. Why do you think they were not ecstatic?

d. As Jesus continued walking with the men, they reached their destination. It was customary during those days to be hospitable and invite a traveling stranger to have dinner at your home, and perhaps even spend the night. It was also customary for the stranger not to assume such hospitality, but act as though he were going further. Even though Jesus was the guest, He took on the role of the host by breaking the bread and giving thanks. Can you think of any other times in Scripture where Jesus acted similarly?

e. How and when did they finally recognize Jesus? What would they have noticed about His hands as He broke the bread?

4. Immediately, the two men ran to the other disciples, who were hiding behind locked doors. While they were still in the middle of recounting the exciting news of their day, Jesus appeared. Poof, there He was. Let's

take a look at how John recounts the experience. Read John 20:19-31.

   a. What did Jesus show the disciples?

   b. What did Jesus tell the disciples God was calling them to do?

   c. Thomas did not believe the report that Jesus was alive. What did he say was the proof he needed?

   d. Read and describe Thomas' encounter with Jesus in John 20:26-29.

5. Jesus could have very well returned with a resurrected body that had no scars—one that was perfectly healed. Why do you think that He chose to retain the scars from His nailed-pierced hands, feet, and spear-pierced side?

6. In your own life, can you see the beauty of your scars? Yes, God could have left you without them, but they are there for a reason. What are some possible reasons?

7. Record the words of Jesus in John 20:21.

Lesson Three—Reflecting on the Purpose of Our Scars

1. In order to see the purpose of our scars, we have to look at our past from God's perspective. What is God able to do, according to Romans 8:28?

2. Let's look at Paul once again.

   a. Describe Paul's circumstances during the time he wrote the book of Philippians. Especially note the following: Philippians 1:7,17,30; 4:11-14.

b. What was his perspective of what we would call "unfortunate" events in his life? (Philippians 1:12-18)

c. How is Paul an example to us of how not only to survive a difficult situation, but to thrive in a difficult situation?

3. Read Proverbs 25:4-5.

The way a refiner knew that the refining process was finished was when he looked into the silver and saw no dross, but only his reflection. Then he could turn down the heat. As long as the image was murky, he knew he had to keep working. What picture does Malachi 3:3-4 paint in your mind? (The Levites were the men who served God in the tabernacle.)

4. Have you ever felt as though God was turning up the heat in your life to bring some dross to the surface? Explain.

5. Read the following verses and note what you learn about trials:

a. Job 23:10

b. Proverbs 17:3

c. Romans 5:3-5

d. James 1:2-4

e. 1 Peter 1:6-7

6. What conclusion did Job come to at the end of his trials? (Job 42:5)

7. Give an example of something God has taught you through a trial that you might not have learned any other way.

Lesson Four—Redeeming the Pain by Investing in Others

1. Read Isaiah 61:1-3. How has God given you beauty for ashes? Perhaps you still only see the ashes. If so, ask God to show you how He longs to reveal the beauty to you.

2. Read and record 1 Thessalonians 2:8.

3. Read the following verses and note how these people invested in others:

   a. Ruth 1:16; 2:2,11,12

   b. 2 Samuel 9:7-12

   c. Proverbs 31:20

   d. Luke 5:17-19

   e. Luke 10:33-37

4. After Paul met Jesus on the road to Damascus, he spent the rest of his life investing in other people. Let's take a look at one young man in particular:

   a. What did Paul call Timothy?

      i. Romans 16:21

      ii. 1 Corinthians 4:17

      iii. 1 Corinthians 16:10

iv. 2 Corinthians 1:19 (What did Timothy do?)

b. Who were the following letters from?

    i. Philippians 1:1

    ii. 1 Thessalonians 1:1

    iii. 2 Thessalonians 1:1

    iv. Philemon 1:1

c. Where was Paul when he wrote most of these letters? (Philippians 1:13-14; Philemon 1:1)

d. Glance through the books of 1 and 2 Timothy and note how Paul invested in Timothy. Especially note 1Timothy 1:2,18; 6:20; 2 Timothy 1:2.

e. Put yourself in young Timothy's place and imagine how he must have felt toward Paul. Try to put that in words.

5. Read 2 Corinthians 9:6-15.

a. What do you learn about the principle of sowing and reaping?

b. Most think of these passages referring to monetary giving, but how could this also apply to investing in the emotional and spiritual well-being of others?

   c. What is the basis for such giving? (verse15)

6. What did Jesus do to invest in others? (Mark 10:45)

7. Is there someone that God wants you to invest in today?

Lesson Five—Replacing the Wounds with Scars

1. Sometimes our wounds can feel like an unmovable mountain. Whether it is something that was done to us or through us, God can remove the pain and the shame. What we see as impossible, God sees as done. Read Zechariah 4:6-7 and answer the following questions:

   a. Zerubbabel was concerned about his ability to rebuild the temple of God. What was the angel's reply in verse 6?

   b. Often in the Bible, obstacles are viewed as mountains. What does verse 7 say that God can do to the obstacles in our lives that stand in the way of us obeying God?

   c. A capstone is the final stone, signifying the completion of a project. What will be the shouts of praise after the obstacle is leveled and the capstone is in place? If you have access to a New American Standard version, record those words as well.

   d. It is grace that levels the mountain of our sin. How has God's grace leveled the mountain of your sin?

   e. Do you realize that your sin has been removed, or are you constantly going back with a bucket and a shovel trying to put the mountain back in place?

2. Not convinced? Let's look at a few other verses about God leveling the mountains in our lives. Read the following verses and note what you

learn about God's power to remove obstacles in our path to obedience:

a. Isaiah 40:1-5

b. Look up and record the definition of "prepare."

c. Are there mountains and valleys in your life that need to be leveled before you can walk the path that God has for you? If so, what are they?

d. Are you willing?

e. What does verse 5 tell us will be the outcome?

3. Isaiah 49:11-13 also uses the imagery of leveling mountains and raising up valleys to remove the obstacles in our lives. Read these verses and note:

a. Who will come, once the obstacles are removed?

b. What is God's purpose for the people coming?

c. Do you believe that God can use your life to comfort His people?

d. Are there obstacles that need to be removed in order for that to happen?

4. Let's look at a few New Testament verses on mountain removal. Read and note what you learn from the following:

a. Matthew 17:20

   b. Matthew 21:21-22

   c. Mark 11:23-25

   d. 1 Corinthians 13:2

5. Once you have asked God to remove the obstacles in your way, whether it is forgiving yourself, forgiving the one who hurt you, your lack of faith, your shame, your embarrassment, your fear, etc., accept it and be done with it. The capstone was the final stone and signified the work was finished. What were Jesus' final words on the cross? (John 19:30)

Lesson Six—Restoring the Broken Heart

1. Perhaps you have had many bad things happen to you. If so, you are not alone. Let's take a look at how Paul handled abuse and mistreatment. Read 2 Corinthians 11:23-29.

   a. Make a list of all the bad things that happened to Paul.

   b. Did he deserve any of the ill treatment?

   c. How did he handle the ill-treatment? We see his secret in Philippians 3:13-14. What was it?

   d. In Philippians 3:15, what does Paul call Christians who are able to take such a view of our pasts?

   e. Could it be that living in the past keeps us from maturing in Christ?

    f.   Is there something in your past that you need to leave on the side of the road and move past in order to grow into "maturity"?

2. Receiving forgiveness is a big factor in leaving the past behind. Look up and record what you learn about repentance from the following verses:

    a.   Psalm 30:5

    b.   Psalm 51:8

    c.   Psalm 51:14

    d.   Isaiah 57:15

    e.   Isaiah 61:3

    f.   Matthew 6:12

3. What do the following verses say about how God will restore our broken hearts?

    a.   Psalm 30:11-12

    b.   Isaiah 49:4

    c.   Isaiah 61:7-8

    d.   Zechariah 9:11-12

4. How does God feel about those who hurt children? (Luke 17:1-2)

5. What does the Bible say about revenge?

   a. Luke 23:34

   b. Romans 12:19

   c. Romans 12:21

   d. Hebrews 10:30-31

6. What do the following verses tell us about praying for those who hurt us?

   a. Matthew 5:44

   b. Luke 6:28

   c. Romans 12:14

7. Read John 4:1-42. In that culture, only a man could initiate divorce. That means that five times this woman had been rejected by men she had loved. Notice how Jesus treated this woman. How does His tenderness and forgiveness encourage you? What does it tell you about His character? What do you think that Jesus would say to you today about your past?

8. Is there someone that you need to forgive? Why not begin by praying for that person and handing him or her over to God.

Lesson Seven—Receiving Grace and Forgiveness

1. Read the following verses and record what you learn about God's love for you:

   a. Psalm 13:5

   b. Psalm 89:2

   c. Psalm 136

   d. Jeremiah 31:3-4

   e. John 3:16

2. Sin does not have to be a terminal illness. There is a cure! Read the following verses and note the remedy:

   a. John 3:1-21

   b. Romans 10:9

   c. 1 John 1:9

   d. 1 John 4:4

3. Read the following verses and note what you learn about God's forgiveness. Also note the verb tense. Is it present, past, or future?

   a. Ephesians 4:32

　　b.　Colossians 2:13

　　c.　Colossians 3:13

4.　God's grace is one of the key teachings of the New Testament. Read and respond to the following:

　　a.　Using a dictionary, define the word "grace."

　　b.　Moses brought the Law. What did Jesus bring? (John 1:17)

　　c.　What did Paul call the gospel in Acts 20:24?

　　d.　By what are we justified? (Romans 3:24)

　　e.　By what are we saved? (Ephesians 2:8)

　　f.　How do we receive God's grace? (Romans 5:15)

　　g.　This is very key to understanding the grace of God. Read and record what you learn about grace in Romans 11:5-6. Record what verse 6 means to you in your own words.

5.　Now that you have looked at grace and forgiveness, how do you see the two working together?

6.　Read 2 Corinthians 7:10. What is godly sorrow?

7.　Read Luke 18:10-14. Describe these two prayers. Who received mercy?

Why are we slow to show mercy? What does God delight in doing, according to Micah 7:18?

8. Get a piece of paper and write a letter to God explaining exactly what you did. After you have finished, get a red marker and write FORGIVEN across the page or pages.

9. Read and write out Psalm 103:1-5. Highlight or underline the sentences or words that mean the most to you. Now close this lesson by praying Psalm 103 back to God.

Lesson Eight—Renouncing the Cloud of Shame

1. Can you imagine what the Garden of Eden was like without shame, guilt, or fear? Read Genesis 2 and try to describe Adam and Eve's existence without shame.

2. Scan Genesis 3. How did Adam and Eve's relationship with God change once sin entered the world?

3. What was God's plan to remove their shame? (Romans 5:18-19)

4. Adam and Eve tried to cover their shame with fig leaves. What are ways we try to cover or camouflage our shame today?

5. God looked at the fig leaves and knew that they needed something better. Thus God made the first animal sacrifice in order to cover their shame. What do the following verses teach us about Christ's sacrifice to cover our shame and redeem our sins?

   a. Ephesians 1:7-8

   b. Colossians 1:19-20

   c. Hebrews 9:22

   d. Revelation 12:11

6. Read and record Psalm 34:5.

7. Notice the word "covered" in Psalm 34:5. Read the following verses and notice what covers us as a child of God.

   a. Isaiah 61:10

   b. Romans 4:7

8. What is the promise of Romans 10:10-13 in regard to shame?

9. Do you believe that Jesus' sacrifice on the cross was enough to cover and remove your shame?

10. What did Paul say about his own shame in 2 Timothy 1:12?

11. Read 1 Corinthians 6:9-11. List three things in verse 11 that God has done for you.

12. Are you wearing a mantel of shame today, or have you accepted God's gift of righteous robe fit for a princess?

Lesson Nine—Removing the Mask and Being Real

1. Why do you think Christians resist being real or admitting weakness and failures to one another?

2. What do the following verses tell us about how God feels about pride?

   a. Psalm 138:6

   b. Proverbs 3:34

c. James 4:6

d. 1 Peter 5:5

3. Jesus called the Pharisees "whitewashed tombs." Read Matthew 23:27-28. What do you think He meant by that analogy?

4. One of the ways we can encourage others to "be real" is by having a spirit of acceptance and compassion. Read the following verses and note what you learn about creating an environment for openness and honesty:

a. Romans 15:7

b. Colossians 4:6

c. 2 Thessalonians 2:16-17

d. Hebrews 12:15

5. Scan Romans chapter 14. What would you say is the general theme? What is Paul's admonition in 14:4?

6. Is there someone you having been judging harshly? What do you think God would say about our judgmental attitude?

7. Read Galatians 6:1. Why should we be always be merciful to those who have fallen?

8. Read 2 Corinthians 11:3. How did Paul describe their devotion to Christ? Were they mature or new Christians? Now that you have a picture of who he was writing to, what was his warning?

9. Romans 3:23 is the bottom line when it comes to taking off our masks and being real. Read, record, and memorize this verse.

Lesson Ten—Resisting the Fear of Rejection

1. When it comes to showing our scars, we may be embarrassed by our apparent weakness. What does Paul say about his weaknesses in the following verses?

   a. Romans 8:26-27

   b. 1 Corinthians 1:27

   c. 1 Corinthians 2:3-4

   d. 2 Corinthians 12:9-10

2. What was God's comment to the prophet Samuel about the people's rejection? (1 Samuel 8:7)

3. Almost every leader in the Bible faced rejection at one point in his life. Look up the following verses and fill in the blanks.

   a. Joseph was rejected by _____. (Genesis 37:5-8,18-25)

   b. Moses was rejected by _____ . (Acts 7:33-36)

   c. Moses was also rejected by _____. (Numbers 12:1-3)

d. David was rejected by _____ . (1 Samuel 17:28)

e. David was also rejected by _____. (1 Samuel 18:5-12)

f. Paul and Silas were rejected by _____. (Acts 16:16-26)

4. The greatest rejection in recorded history occurred when man rejected the Son of God. What do the following verses teach us about Jesus?

a. Isaiah 53:3

b. Matthew 21:42

c. Mark 8:31

5. Read what the following verses have to say about being "men pleasers."

a. Galatians 1:10

b. Ephesians 6:6

c. Colossians 3:17

d. Colossians 3:23

6. First Peter 2:4 holds the key to victory over rejection. Fill in the blanks:

"As you come to him, the living Stone—rejected by _____ but chosen by _____.

7. What are the promises and rewards in spite of possible rejection? (Luke 6:22-23)

8. Can you think of scars in your life that you are hiding because of the fear of rejection?

Lesson Eleven—Rejecting the Lie of Disqualification

1. Sometimes we can feel as though we are the only ones who have made bad decisions, been abused, or failed. What do the following verses tell us about our collective propensity to sin?

   a. Isaiah 53:6

   b. Romans 3:10

   c. Romans 7:18

   From these verses, who do you think would be qualified to serve God because of their own merit?

2. When it comes to judging others or others judging us, God has some definite opinions of both. Read the following and note what you learn about people judging people:

   a. Matthew 7:1-2

   b. Romans 14:4

   c. 1 Corinthians 4: 3-4

   d. James 4:12

3. Read Matthew 7:3-6 and paraphrase these words in your own words.

4. When we come to Christ, we are a new creation. Read and record what you learn about your new life in Christ:

   a. Romans 8:1

   b. 2 Corinthians 5:17

   c. Galatians 2:20

   d. Colossians 1:13-14

   e. Colossians 1:21-23

5. What did the angel tell Peter to teach in the temple in Acts 5:20?

6. What does Colossians 1:12 say about your qualifications as a child of God?

7. What is standing in your way of believing that God has qualified you to be His child, a chosen ambassador for Him, or equipped for ministry?

Lesson Twelve—Revealing the Truth

1. It would have been very easy for God to have left out the less honorable qualities of the heroes in the Bible. However, He chose to include the good, the bad, and the ugly characteristics of his chosen servants. Today, we will look at several familiar men and women in the Bible. Make two columns on a piece of paper and complete the following chart.

	Positive Character Trait	Shortcomings
Noah	Genesis 6:8	Genesis 9:21
Abraham	Genesis 15:6	Genesis 12:1-13
Sarah	Genesis 21:1-2	Genesis 16:1-2
Isaac	Genesis 26:28	Genesis 26:7
Rebekah	Genesis 24:15-21	Genesis 27:5-13
Jacob	Genesis 25:23	Genesis 27:18-19
David	1 Samuel 16:13; Acts 13:22	2 Samuel 11:1-26
Solomon	1 Kings 3:7-15	1 Kings 11:1-6

2. Why do you think God made sure to record the failures as well as the successes of His chosen people? (1 Corinthians 10:6,11)

3. What does Romans 3:10 tell us about our life without Christ?

4. Look up and define the word "redeem."

5. What do the following verses teach you about "being redeemed"?

   a. Deuteronomy 7:8-9

   b. Deuteronomy 24:18

   c. Job 33:28

   d. Isaiah 43:1-2

   e. 1 Peter 1:18-19

6. If you are a Christian, then you have been redeemed or bought back. What have you been redeemed from? Be specific.

7. What did Jesus tell us to do with the light that is with us? (Matthew 5:14-15)

8. Brennan Manning said, "The essence of messy spirituality is the refusal to pretend, to lie, or to allow others to believe we are something we are not."

   a. Are there areas where you have pretended to be different than you really are?

   b. How could being real and revealing the truth help others to understand redemption?

   c. Are you willing to remove your mask and reveal the truth in order to lead others to the Truth—Jesus Christ?

Lesson Thirteen—Releasing the Power of Our Scars

Paul was a man who had many scars, both emotionally and physically. Let's look at his struggles and how he used them to glorify God.

1. Read 2 Corinthians 4:7-18 and answer the following questions:

   a. Make a list of the contrasts in these verses.
   Example: pressed on every side—but not crushed (verse 8)

   b. What did "believing" compel Paul to do? Also note 1 Corinthians 9:16.

   c. Do your beliefs compel you to speak? If so, why? If not, why not?

   d. What is the benefit of speaking out found in verse 15?

e. Paul's suffering was undoubtedly taking a toll on his physical body. How does Paul compare the struggle of this world to the rewards that are yet to come?

f. Suffering resulting in glory did not happen automatically. Paul had to keep his focus on Christ and decide what was paramount. How did he do this? Also see Colossians 3:1-2.

g. What are some ways we can "fix our eyes on what is unseen" rather than focusing on what is seen?

h. In which realm do you spend most of your thoughts and energy—the seen or unseen?

2. Read 1 Peter 4:12-13,19.

a. What do these verses tell you about the inevitability of suffering?

b. What do the verses tell us about how we are to react?

c. Why should we rejoice in suffering?

d. Paul was trying to encourage new believers, yet these don't seem like very encouraging words. Why do you suppose he wanted them to have this perspective on suffering?

e. Are there some scars in your own life you could regard differently with this perspective?

f. Jesus taught His disciples about suffering. What did He say in John 16:33?

g. What did Paul see as the benefit of his suffering? (2 Corinthians 12:9-10)

h. How could your scar or suffering be beneficial for you?

3. Read Acts 16:25-34 and answer the following questions:

a. Where were Paul and Silas?

b. What were they doing?

c. What happened as they were singing?

d. What effect did their freedom have on the jailer?

e. What effect could your "freedom" have on those who know your story?

4. What happened when the following people revealed what God had done for them?

a. Matthew 9:6-8

b. Matthew 9:28-31

c. Mark 5:18-19

d. John 4:39

e. Acts 3:7-9

5. Have you ever thought that you are an actual representative of Jesus here on earth? Read the following verses and note your role:

a. 2 Corinthians 2:15

b. 2 Corinthians 3:3

c. 2 Corinthians 3:18

d. 2 Corinthians 5:20

6. What is your story? Are you ready to experience the power of God working through your life as you share with others what God has done for you?

7. Read and record 1 Corinthians 2:9!

Notes

Chapter 2—Recognizing Jesus Through Our Scars
1. John 9:1-11 MSG.
2. John 9:18-21 MSG.
3. John 9: 24-25 MSG.
4. Rick Warren, *The Purpose-Driven Life* (Grand Rapids, MI: Zondervan Publishers, 2002), p. 290.

Chapter 3—Reflecting on the Purpose of Our Scars
1. James Dobson, *When God Doesn't Make Sense* (Wheaton, IL: Tyndale House Publishers, 1993), p. 8.

Chapter 4—Redeeming the Pain by Investing in Others
1. Beth Moore, *The Patriarchs* (Nashville, TN: Lifeway Press, 2005), p. 158.
2. Dan Clark, *Puppies for Sale and Other Inspirational Tales* (Deerfield Beach, FL: Health Communications, Inc., 1997), p. 3. Used by permission of Health Communications, Inc.
3. Philip Yancey, *Where Is God When It Hurts?* (Grand Rapids, MI: Zondervan Publishers, 1990), p. 157.

Chapter 5—Replacing the Wounds with Scars
1. *Zondervan NIV Commentary, Volume 2, New Testament* (Grand Rapids, MI: Zondervan Publishers, 1994), p. 806.
2. Richard Exley, as quoted by Carol Kent in *When I Lay My Isaac Down* (Colorado Springs, CO: NavPress Publishing Group, 2004), p. 33.
3. Neil Anderson, *Victory Over the Darkness* (Ventura, CA: Regal Books, 1990), p. 188.
4. *Webster's Dictionary of the English Language* (New York, NY: Lexicon Publications, Inc., 1990), p. 797.
5. U.S. Department of Justice, Office of Justice Programs, Bureau of Justice Statistics Special Report, "Recidivism of Prisoners Released in 1994," June 2002, NCJ 193427.

Chapter 6—Restoring the Broken Heart
1. Florence Littauer, *Silver Boxes* (Dallas, TX: W Publishing Group, 1989), p. 74.
2. Susan Forward, *Toxic Parents* (New York, NY: Bantam Books, 1989), p. 48.
3. Ibid., p. 11.
4. Ibid., p. 159.
5. David Seamands, *Healing of Memories* (New York, NY: Inspiration Press, 1985), p. 360.
6. Forward, *Toxic Parents,* p. 140.

7. Diane Dempsey Marr, *The Reluctant Traveler* (Colorado Springs, CO: NavPress Publishing Group, 2002), p. 113.

8. Spiros Zodhiates, et al., eds., *The Complete Word Study Dictionary: New Testament* (Chattanooga, TN: AMG Publishers, 1992), p. 229.

9. Ron Lee Davis, *Mistreated* (Portland, OR: Multnomah Press, 1989), p. 84–86.

Chapter 7—Receiving Grace and Forgiveness

1. Diane Dempsey Marr, *The Reluctant Traveler* (Colorado Springs, CO: NavPress Publishing Group, 2002), p. 155.

2. Brennan Manning, *The Ragamuffin Gospel* (Sisters, OR: Multnomah Publishers, Inc., 1990), p. 26.

3. Special thanks to Charles Chandler of *The Charlotte Observer* for the series of articles printed July 11, 12, 13, 2004 ("Forgiving Karl," July 11, 2004, pp. 1A and 8A; July 12, 2004, pp. 1A and 8A; and July 13, 2004, pp. 1A and 6A). Many of the details of Karl's trial were gleaned from Chandler's articles. Used by permission of the author.

4. Manning, *The Ragamuffin Gospel*, p. 78.

5. Ibid., p. 114.

6. C.S. Lewis, *Miracles* (San Francisco, CA: HarperSanFrancisco, a division of HarperCollins Publishers, 1947, HarperCollins edition 2001), p. 198.

7. Ken Gire, *Windows of the Soul* (Grand Rapids, MI: Zondervan Publishers, 1996), p. 194.

8. W.E. Vine, Merrill F. Unger, William White Jr., *Vine's Complete Expository Dictionary of Old and New Testament Words* (Nashville, TN: Thomas Nelson Publishers, 1985), p. 250.

9. Ibid., p. 120.

10. Ibid., p. 525.

11. Beth Moore, *When Godly People Do Ungodly Things* (Nashville, TN: Lifeway Press, 2003), p. 145.

12. Joyce Meyer, *Beauty from Ashes* (Tulsa, OK: Harrison House, 1994), p. 75.

Chapter 8—Renouncing the Cloud of Shame

1. Beth Moore, *When Godly People Do Ungodly Things* (Nashville, TN: LifeWay Press, 2003), p. 86.

2. Lysa TerKeurst, *Who Holds the Key to Your Heart?* (Chicago, IL: Moody Publishers, 2002), p. 18.

3. Bob and Audrey Meisner, *Marriage Undercover* (Huntsville, AL: Milestones International Publishers, 2005), p. 138.

Chapter 9—Removing the Mask and Being Real

1. C.S. Lewis, *The Lion, the Witch, and the Wardrobe* (New York, NY: Collier, 1950), p. 137.

2. Michael Yaconelli, *Messy Spirituality* (Grand Rapids, MI: Zondervan Publishers, 2002), pp. 16–17.

3. Keith Miller, as quoted by Michael Yaconelli in *Messy Spirituality*, pp. 22-23.

4. Yaconelli, *Messy Spirituality*, p. 27.

5. Brennan Manning, *The Ragamuffin Gospel* (Sisters, OR: Multnomah Publishers, Inc., 1990), p. 30.

6. Nancy Leigh DeMoss, *Brokenness—The Heart God Revives* (Chicago, IL: Moody Publishers, 2002), p. 94.

7. Margery Williams, *The Velveteen Rabbit* (New York, NY: Doubleday & Company, Inc., no date), p. 16-17.

8. DeMoss, *Brokenness,* p. 123.

9. Brenda Waggoner, *The Velveteen Woman* (Colorado Springs, CO: Chariot Victor Publishing, 1999), p. 19.

Chapter 11—Rejecting the Lie of Disqualification

1. Beth Moore, *When Godly People Do Ungodly Things* (Nashville, TN: LifeWay Press, 2003), pp. 118-19.

2. Michael Yaconelli, *Messy Spirituality* (Grand Rapids, MI: Zondervan Publishers, 2002), pp. 69-70.

3. Rick Reilly, "Half the Size, Twice the Man," *Sports Illustrated,* October 3, 2005, p. 90.

Chapter 12—Revealing the Truth

1. Bob and Audrey Meisner, *Marriage Undercover* (Huntsville, AL: Milestones International Publishers, 2005), p. 26.

2. Ibid., p. 68.

3. Nancy Leigh DeMoss, *Brokenness—The Heart God Revives* (Chicago, IL: Moody Publishers, 2002), pp. 111-12.

4. Ibid., pp. 26-27.

5. Brennan Manning, *The Ragamuffin Gospel* (Sisters, OR: Multnomah Publishers, 1990), p. 134.

6. *Real Simple,* September 2005, p. 47.

7. Brennan Manning, as quoted by Carol Kent in *When I Lay My Isaac Down* (Colorado Springs, CO: NavPress Publishing Group, 2004), p. 159.

8. Melissa Healy, "Friendship's Healing Power," *The Charlotte Observer,* May 30, 2005, Section E, p. 1.

9. Ibid., p. 3.

10. Pam Vredevelt, *Letting Go of Disappointments and Painful Losses* (Sisters, OR: Multnomah Publishers, Inc., 2001), p. 17.

11. Sheila Walsh, *Honestly* (Grand Rapids, MI: Zondervan Publishers, 1996), p. 48.

12. Ibid., p. 102.

13. C.S. Lewis, *Mere Christianity* (Westwood, NJ: Barbour and Company, Inc., no date), p. 168.

14. Neil Anderson, *Victory Over the Darkness* (Ventura, CA: Regal Books, 1990), p. 203.

15. Beth Moore, as quoted by Jane Johnson Struck in "Beth's Passion," *Today's Christian Woman,* September/October 2005, pp. 32-33.

Chapter 13—Releasing the Power of Our Scars

1. Henry Pierson Curtis, "Blemish for Navy Officer," *The Orlando Sentinel,* November 6, 1999, p. 1.

2. Excerpted from *When I Lay My Isaac Down* by Carol Kent, copyright 2004 (pp. 16-17). Used by permission of NavPress—www.navpress.com. All rights reserved.

3. Ibid., p. 24.

4. Ibid., p. 72.

5. Ibid., p. 125.

6. Ibid., pp. 175, 178-79.

7. W.E. Vine, Merrill F. Unger, William White Jr., *Vine's Complete Expository Dictionary of Old and New Testament Words* (Nashville, TN: Thomas Nelson Publishers, 1985), p. 478.

8. Nancy Leigh DeMoss, *Brokenness—The Heart God Revives* (Chicago, IL: Moody Publishers, 2002), pp. 49-50.

About the Author

Sharon Jaynes is an international inspirational speaker and Bible teacher for women's conferences and events. She is also the author of several books, including *Becoming the Woman of His Dreams, Becoming a Woman Who Listens to God, Becoming Spiritually Beautiful,* and *Dreams of a Woman: God's Plans for Fulfilling Your Dreams.* Her books have been translated into several foreign languages and impacted women all around the globe. Sharon and her husband, Steve, live in North Carolina and have one grown son, Steven.

Sharon is always honored to hear from her readers. Please write to her directly at:

Sharon@sharonjaynes.com
or at her mailing address:

Sharon Jaynes
P.O. Box 725
Matthews, North Carolina 28106

To learn more about Sharon's books and speaking ministry or to inquire about having Sharon speak at your next event, visit www.sharonjaynes.com.